JAN TSCHICHOLD: A LIFE IN TYPOGRAPHY

SOUTHAMPTON
INSTITUTE

Ruari McLean

Jan Tschichold

A Life in Typography

Lund Humphries Publishers • London

First published in 1997 by
Lund Humphries Publishers Ltd
Park House, 1 Russell Gardens
London NW11 9NN

British Library Cataloguing in Publication Data:
A catalogue record for this book is available from the British Library.

ISBN 0 85331 668 6

Typeset in Sabon.
Designed by Chrissie Charlton & Company.
Origination in the UK, printing and binding in Singapore, all under the supervision
of MRM Graphics.

Frontispiece:
Jan Tschichold at the Leipzig Academy, 1920.

CONTENTS

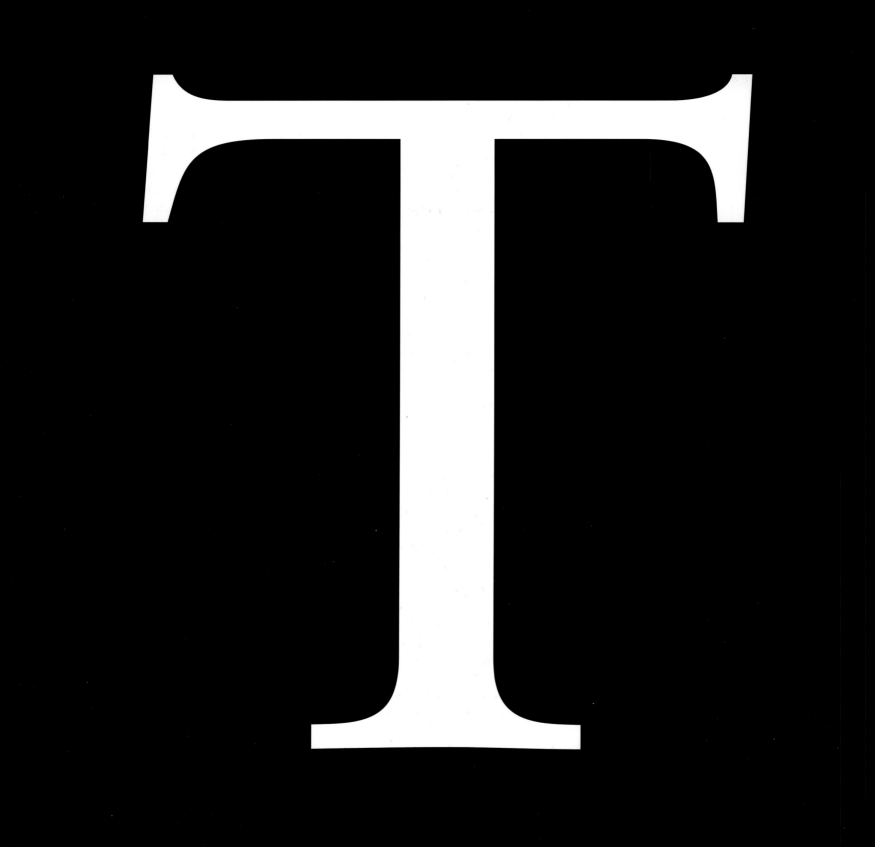

JAN TSCHICHOLD:
A LIFE IN TYPOGRAPHY

Jan Tschichold made two unique contributions to the history and practice of typography.

The first was that, as a young design student, he saw and was inspired by the modern movement proclaimed by Walter Gropius and the Bauhaus in Weimar in 1923. Tschichold showed – as no-one in the Bauhaus had done – how the new ideas could be used to improve the design of ordinary, day-to-day printing. This could only be achieved, he said at the time, by asymmetrical design and sanserif type. But he never forgot that the real purpose of typography is communication.

The second was when, having been hounded out of Germany by the Nazis as a preacher of what they called '*Kultur-Bolschewismus*', and working first in Switzerland and then in Britain, Tschichold saw that asymmetry was not the only way to design printed matter. The fundamentals of typographic design were much wider. Typography in all its aspects is not only a matter of certain basic laws, but it also and always always depends on the narrowest details. By his practice and teaching, Tschichold's contribution to the typography of the twentieth century was to show the importance of getting all the details right – with elegance.

* * *

Tschichold was born in Leipzig on 2 April 1902, the eldest son of a sign painter and lettering artist. Lettering was therefore something he knew about from his earliest days. He wanted to become an artist, but his parents thought this was too uncertain a career, so he set out to become a teacher of drawing. However, lettering and printing fascinated him. He studied Edward Johnston's *Writing and Illuminating, and Lettering* in the translation of Anna Simons, and works by German lettering artists including Rudolf von Larisch. Gradually he found himself more and more attracted to type design. At the age of seventeen he was enrolled at the Academy for Graphic Arts and Book Production in Leipzig. In 1921, at the age of nineteen, he was appointed by Walter Tiemann (1876-1951), Director of the Leipzig Academy, to be assistant in charge of the evening classes in lettering at the Academy. Examples of Tschichold's lettering from this period show him to have become already both highly skilful and inventive.

In August 1923 he went to see the first Bauhaus exhibition at Weimar. For the first time he saw the work of the 'moderns': Herbert Bayer, Josef Albers,

Marcel Breuer, Feininger, Klee, Moholy-Nagy, El Lissitzky, Kurt Schwitters, Piet Zwart, Man Ray, all the great names of the movement. Tschichold was deeply impressed and immediately committed.

Curiously, the Bauhaus artists tended to use type as a component of abstract art rather than for communication. Their typography was wild, sensational, eye-catching, but in terms of legibility, impractical. They were trying to do other things. It is significant that in the massive 1968 catalogue of the *50 Years Bauhaus* exhibition shown in Stuttgart and London, the typography (by Herbert Bayer) is all in sanserif, and entirely without capital letters – a good example of theory ignoring practicality. Capital letters, like punctuation marks, are functional, since they signal the beginnings of sentences, proper names, different meanings of words, and so on. To omit all capital letters simply makes printed matter a little more difficult to read.

Tschichold, of all the early practitioners of 'modern typography', was the only one whose earliest training was in lettering and calligraphy. He understood better than anyone else what was involved in communication by means of printing. He became the first to offer a coherent philosophy of design by which all typographic problems – not just books, but magazines, newspapers and all the important clutter of day-to-day commercial ephemera – could be tackled in ways that were rational, suited to modern production techniques, and aesthetically satisfying.

From 1925 onwards Tschichold proclaimed his philosophy of typographic design (which at the time was revolutionary) in a series of articles and books. His first publication was in the October 1925 issue of the Leipzig printing periodical *Typographische Mitteilungen* ('Typographic News', see pp. 30-3). It was a special number called 'Elementare Typographie', which he designed and largely wrote himself, under the name of Ivan Tschichold – the artists of Russia being at that time a strong influence. This manifesto, containing ideas completely new to most ordinary printers in Europe, was widely noticed. Then his first book, *Die neue Typographie*, was published in 1928 in Berlin. The text, of considerable importance in the history of typographic thought, was not translated into English until the present writer did so in the late 1960s, and was not published in English until the University of California Press did so in 1995.

The book, written with passionate conviction, reflects its time. Piet Mondrian's words form a preface: *'wir [stehen] an einer Wende der Kultur'*, 'we are at a turning point of civilisation'. Tschichold's first chapter, entitled 'The new world-view', contains the words 'Instead of recognizing and designing for the laws of machine production, the previous generation contented itself with trying anxiously to follow a tradition that was in any case only imaginary. Before them stand the works of today, untainted by the past, primary shapes which identify the aspect of our time: Car Aeroplane Telephone Wireless Factory Neon-advertising New York! These objects, designed without reference to the aesthetics of the past, have been created by a new kind of man: **the engineer!**'

The whole book must be read to grasp Tschichold's vision, but we may also quote (from page 68 in the English translation): 'Asymmetry is the rhythmic expression of functional design' and 'The liveliness of asymmetry is also an expression of our own movement and that of modern life'. Of type, he writes (pp. 75-8): 'I find the best face in use today is the so-called ordinary jobbing sanserif, which is quiet and easy to read' (and in which the book is set). Also: 'We require from type plainness, clarity, the rejection of everything that is superfluous'. But on page 75 he also says, in relation to 'national scripts, which contradict present day transnational bonds between people', 'Roman type is the international typeface of the future'.

Not only the text but also the design of *Die neue Typographie* is of outstanding interest. It was not intended as a fine limited edition, but as a working text for compositors and printers. Nevertheless it has both elegance and originality, qualities which recur in nearly everything that Tschichold designed. The flexible case, in black linen with silver blocking on the spine, is pleasant to touch. The text pages, in a contemporary (non-artist-designed) sanserif, are printed on a non-shiny, slightly off-white text paper. The typography is not assertive (as was so much Bauhaus typography) but expressive and practical; and the book begins unforgettably with a solid black frontispiece. The book was reprinted in facsimile in Berlin in 1987; the binding is just a fraction stiffer, the paper just a little too white and shiny, the whole effect just missing the subtle qualities of the first edition.

Tschichold continued writing and designing, not only books but all kinds of printing, including the now famous series of film posters for the Phoebus-Palast Cinema in Munich (see pp. 38-9).

In the few years between 1928 and 1933, Tschichold was formulating a completely new philosophy of typographic design. How different it was from what had gone before can be seen when it is compared with the best work being done at that time in England by, for example, Stanley Morison, Oliver Simon and Francis Meynell.

Then the Nazis struck. The new typography and the modern movement in art became a political issue in Germany and was labelled decadent – a feeling, it must be remembered, not without its supporters in England. The Nazis wanted Germany's printing and lettering to be in black letter. Tschichold's teaching post in Munich was cancelled, and he and his wife were placed in 'protective custody' – she for a few days, he for six weeks. Tschichold, not being a Jew, was allowed to emigrate. In 1933 he moved with his wife and young son to Switzerland, where he had been offered a small retainer by a publisher in Basel, Benno Schwabe.

For the first few years in Switzerland Tschichold was in a fairly precarious position: there was the constant fear of losing his work permit and even permission to stay in Switzerland. His work was almost entirely confined to designing books, and he found that the asymmetry he had been preaching was not much liked by the conventional Swiss and was often actually unsuitable. He began to realise that in typographic design, asymmetry and symmetry are not mutually exclusive philosophies but different ways of achieving the same end: they can and must live together.

In Autumn 1935 his next (actually, his sixth) book was published by Benno Schwabe, *Typographische Gestaltung* ('Typographic Design', see pp. 50-1). It is as elegant in production as *Die neue Typographie*, but shows significant developing ideas in design. The text is set not in sanserif but in a small size of Bodoni, well leaded, and the title page is set in three contrasting faces: the author's name in a script, the title in an Egyptian (Trump's City), and the publisher in Bodoni. City is also used throughout for headings. The text gives a most valuable account of the art of typography, accepting both symmetric (centred) and asymmetric design. The book was soon translated into Danish, Swedish and Dutch, but not into English: that had to wait until 1967 and the sponsorship of an enlightened typesetting firm in Toronto. In England in 1935, typography, when it was thought about at all, was firmly rooted in tradition, as practised by Morison, Simon and Meynell. The modern movement, in art and architecture as well as typography, was familiar to only a few. Nevertheless, Tschichold's work was beginning to be noticed. At the suggestion of McKnight Kauffer, the great American designer then practising in London, Tschichold was invited to have a small exhibition of his work in the London office of Lund Humphries, at that time one of the most technically advanced and forward-looking printers in the country. Two years later, he was even invited to read a paper on 'A new approach to typography' to the Double Crown Club in London. But the design of the dinner menu (see p.54), always an important feature of these occasions, shows a childish misunderstanding of Tschichold's subject. His new approach was, however, clearly shown in the design of *The Penrose Annual* made for Lund Humphries in 1938.

Tschichold continued during the war to design books for Swiss publishers. His most important commission was the Birkhäuser classics, a series in pocket size for which he designed some fifty-three titles. These were seen and admired in London by Oliver Simon. Tschichold was now also enhancing his reputation with a number of authoritative illustrated books on the history of lettering and typography, in particular *Geschichte der Schrift in Bildern* in 1941 (republished as *An Illustrated History of Writing and Lettering* by Zwemmer in London in 1946), and a splendid landscape volume of 200 plates, *Schatzkammer der Schreibkunst*, in 1945.

* * *

Penguin Books were first published in 1935. It is difficult now to imagine what these paperback novels at sixpence each meant to younger people (and older ones too) who up until then could only afford to borrow the books they wanted to read. During the world war that followed, they proved to be an unbelievable blessing to the troops, and to civilians. They could be carried in gas-mask bags, and often the gas-mask was left out to accommodate more Penguins. When the war was over, Allen Lane, Penguin's founder, had a fast growing business to organise and had the genius to realise that he needed not just any designer, but the best in the world that he could buy. Where could he find that person? He asked many people, including the present writer, and we all replied that there were plenty of good designers in this country, that there was no need to go abroad. Oliver Simon recommended Jan Tschichold. Allen Lane, as on many other occasions, rejected the advice of the majority. He and Oliver Simon crossed to Switzerland and engaged Tschichold to become the Penguin typographical supremo. He arrived in March 1947.

Before he came over, Tschichold asked for a copy of every single piece of printed paper used by Penguin, as well as examples of all their books. By that time, over 500 different titles had been published as Penguins, and there were also King Penguins, Pelicans, Puffins, and several other series on the way. Tschichold annotated every item with his criticisms in pencil. These comments, circulated to editorial staff before he arrived, were a typographical education in themselves.

His task when he arrived was formidable. The standards of composition in English printing-houses were, he found, much lower than in Switzerland. 'The printers who set the type either had no composition rules at all, or worked to nineteenth-century conventions, or followed one set or another of house rules.' One of the first things he did was to write Penguin Composition Rules, a four-page leaflet now famous and of crucial importance (see pp.80-1). He had endless trouble with the hand-compositors who worked on title pages: 'They simply could not understand what I meant by "Capitals must be letter-spaced".' Many printers tried to rebel; but if, as happened, they argued with Tschichold, he produced a bland smile and could not understand English. He was the boss.

An argument once occurred with an author. Dorothy Sayers, creator of the detective Lord Peter Wimsey, had been one of Allen Lane's first ten authors. Later, she translated Dante's *Inferno*, to be published by Penguin in 1949 (see p.94). She objected to three asterisks on her title page, and wrote to Tschichold about it – daring lady. He wrote back: '...As you already know, I have not followed your suggestion to take out the little asterisks...In your letter you express the opinion that no self-respecting title page should ever carry an asterisk. I wonder where you learnt this, but in any case it is the master who establishes the rules and not the pupil, and the master is permitted to break the rules, even his own. These asterisks are necessary in order to emphasize the centre of the composition, to avoid incoherence and to establish a suitable interruption between the three upper parts. The third asterisk is necessary to complete the shape of the upper half.'

Sayers replied by return of post: '... The objection to the asterisks and the three-em rule as ornament is, I think, that they are not primarily designed to fulfil this function, but to perform other duties (such as punctuation and so forth), and therefore have a weak and improvised appearance when set to do a job for which they were not intended.' Tschichold replied: 'I have not used the asterisk in this instance to disguise an error in proportion. It is of real importance in the construction of my title, and to relinquish the asterisk is to weaken its perfection...we shall leave the title as it is.' She replied: 'It's quite all right. I told Mr Overton that if you felt passionate about your little asterisks I didn't <u>really</u> mind; and the editor says you may have them, so everything in the garden is lovely. If anyone cavils at them, I shall explain that they are deeply symbolical and refer to threefold repetition of the word *stelle*, one at the end of each cantica!' Tschichold answered: 'Thank you for your letter. Your book is now on the point of being returned to the printers, and I hope when you see the finished result you will be reconciled to my obstinacy.'

* * *

Tschichold's achievement at Penguin Books was unique. Probably no other man in the world at that time could have achieved what he did. It required a tireless attention to detail, an unshakable belief in the rightness of his own principles, an ability to systematise and to remain consistently faithful to the systems, and a thick skin.

He had done more, in three years, to improve the standards of British book production than any other single book designer had ever done. Although he laid down standards for every detail of Penguin layout (for numerous different series) that were needed, he never standardised either the typeface or the layout of title pages. Every book was treated as a separate design problem and was given a solution that fitted that particular text. The one thing that Tschichold found excellent in British printing was the range of monotype typefaces planned by Morison.

In December 1949 Tschichold returned to Switzerland, leaving behind his monument in every bookshop in the world that sold British books – for Penguins, now produced in quantities of more than fifteen million books a year, would have been in every one.

Back in Switzerland, Tschichold resumed design work for various Swiss and German publishers. In 1954 he was asked to become head of the Munich Academy of Graphic Arts (from which he had been expelled in 1933) but this would have meant returning to live in Germany, and he declined.

In 1955 he became consultant to the large pharmaceutical firm of F. Hoffman-La Roche in Basel, and designed their entire range of books, labels, advertisements and stationery. This included a series of booklets explaining the uses of new drugs to the medical profession, in German, French and/or English, illustrated with photographs and line drawings often in several colours. They are essentially restrained in style (some would say they are actually 'under-designed' – better than being 'over-designed') but with all of Tschichold's meticulous attention to detail. Mostly set in Garamond and printed on toned Basingwerk Parchment, they do not carry the names of either designer or printer.

In 1960, Otto Maier in Ravensburg published *Erfreuliche Drucksachen durch gute Typographie* – 'Pleasant printed matter through good typography' – a handbook in which Tschichold aimed to teach the public (not students, compositors or printers) what good lettering and typography is all about. An excellent idea, it was never translated into English; but modern printing technology soon made much of its background obsolete.

Tschichold's last important typographical commission was to design a new typeface. A group of German master printers decided that they required a type that would appear the same whether it was set by hand from foundry type or machine-set by Monotype or Linotype, and could therefore be interchanged. It should also be easy and pleasant to read and suitable for all printing purposes. Something like Garamond was suggested, but approximately five per cent narrower, and it should be available in roman, italic, and semi-bold. 'Such a brief', observed John Dreyfus in the *Penrose Annual* of 1968, 'to many type designers would have appeared not merely daunting but dispiriting.' Tschichold was given the commission and performed it with enthusiasm and skill. The new type, christened 'Sabon', was manufactured in Frankfurt. It was first used in 1966 and was immediately and widely praised. Sebastian Carter, in his *Twentieth Century Type Designers*, writes of it: 'Sabon is an admirable face, strong yet restrained…The roman capitals in particular are so handsome that one regrets that no titling fount was produced…' Tschichold's drawings for Sabon, with his own annotations, have been occasionally reproduced and are a typographical education in themselves.

From early in his career, Tschichold was greatly interested in Japanese and more especially Chinese calligraphy and printing. In 1940 he published *Der frühe chinesische Farbendruck* ('Early Chinese Colour Printing'), and one of his last published books contained beautiful colour reproductions of Chinese colour printing: *Die Bildersammlung der Zehnbambushalle* (Rentsch, Switzerland, 1970), published in English in 1972 by Lund Humphries as *Chinese Colour Prints from the Ten Bamboo Studio*.

Tschichold's scholarship in this subject (as in so many others) was immense. He researched it in the British Museum whenever he was in London, and I remember his astonishment when we found that Robert van Gulik, one of his most respected authorities on Chinese colour printing, was also the author of my then favourite series of thrillers about Judge Dee.

A minor but rewarding activity during these years was Tschichold's ability to persuade firms to sponsor reproductions, often in colour and in large sizes, of graphic work of historical importance, for giving away as New Year gifts, both by Edith and Jan and by the firm concerned. A fine example was entitled 'The oldest printed poster made for an established tradesman: Paris, *circa* 1560'. It measured 386 x 275 mm and reproduced a poster engraved in wood or metal for a Parisian milliner and hosier, Pierre Baudeau. Tschichold had found it poorly reproduced in an old bookseller's catalogue, where its importance had not been realised. From internal evidence he dated it to about 1560, 'in the period when silk stockings, which had hitherto been worn only at court, were gradually becoming generally fashionable'. It was now reproduced, with Tschichold's retouching, at its true size in both black-and-white and heightened with eight printed colours: the original would certainly have been hand-coloured. The generous sponsor of this magnificent 'trifle' was Clichés Schwitter, Basel & Zurich. Versions were printed in both German and English (see p. 120).

Like all good typographers Tschichold collected printed ephemera, including old engraved trade cards, modern orange papers and Victoriana. He had a special and valuable collection of early writing books, and also collected any scraps of old paper he could find, which he used, when suitable, for repairing the torn page of a sixteenth- or seventeenth-century writing book. These he could repair with professional skill.

In 1968 the Tschicholds left Basel and moved everything to a small house in the Tessin Italian-speaking area of Switzerland above Locarno, facing south, which they had previously built and used as a holiday home. The house had a beautiful, small garden and three separate book-lined rooms used by Tschichold as studies. They are shown as photographs in *Leben und Werk des Typographen Jan Tschichold*, published by Verlag der Kunst, Dresden in 1977.

Jan Tschichold died of cancer in Locarno Hospital on 11 August 1974 – sadly early, but with many honours and a lifetime's work that is still being more and more widely appreciated.

PLATES

Calligraphic New Year wishes, 1920.
Etching, actual size. In 1920 Tschichold was
eighteen: his skill as a calligrapher from an
early age was remarkable.

sich: die Jagdhunde sprangen und wedelten,
die Tauben auf dem Dache zogen das Köpf-
chen unterm Flügel hervor, sahen umher
und flogen ins Feld; die Fliegen an den Wän-
den krochen weiter; das Feuer in der Küche
erhob sich, flackerte und kochte das Essen:
der Braten fing wieder an zu brutzeln: und
der Koch gab dem Jungen eine Ohrfeige daß
er schrie: und die Magd rupfte das Huhn
fertig. Und da wurde die Hochzeit des Königs-
sohns mit dem Dornröschen in aller Pracht
gefeiert, und sie lebten vergnügt bis an ihr
Ende

Johannes Tschichhold scrib. Lipsiae 1920

Leipziger Messe

Allgemeine Mustermesse mit
Technischer Messe und
Baumesse

Die allgemeine internationale
Messe Deutschlands

Die erste und größte Messe der Welt.
Für Aussteller und Einkäufer
gleich wichtig.

Beginn der Herbstmesse am 27. August 1922.

Auskunft erteilt und Anmeldungen nimmt entgegen
Messamt für die Mustermessen
in Leipzig

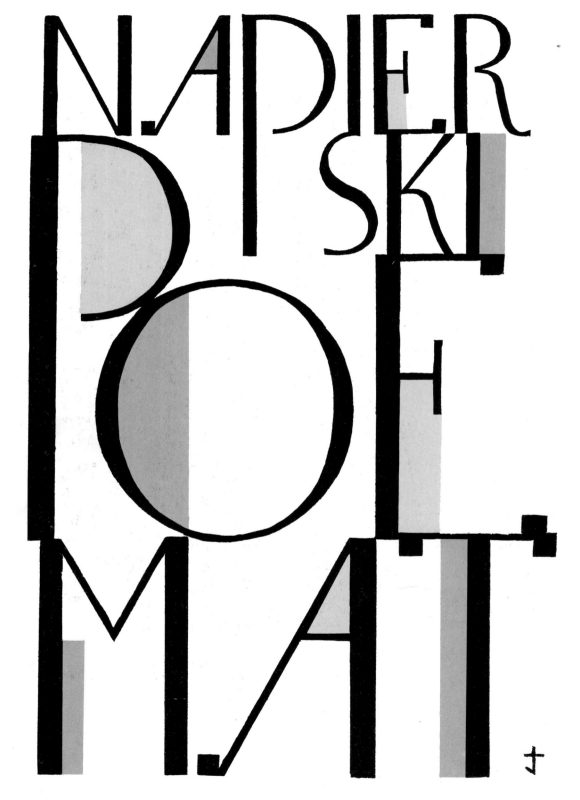

DIE IDEE UND DAS EWIGE SIND DAS MASSGEBENDE NICHT IRGEND EIN MENSCH ODER IRGEND EINE ZEIT

Lettering, reduced, 1923. Original in black only. The interweaving of the letters is amazing and successful.

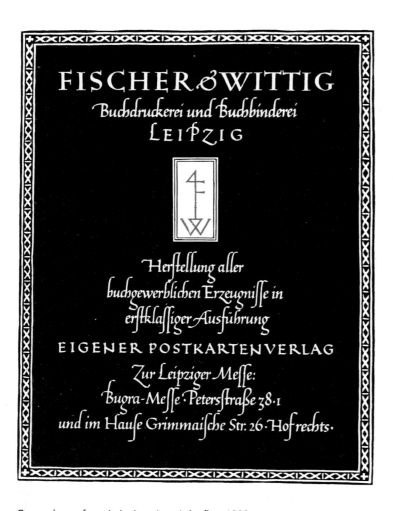

Cover drawn for a Leipzig printer's leaflet, 1923,
based on studies of Arrighi's and Tagliente's
writing-books.

25 Jahre
Insel-Verlag
1899 - 1924

IT

Advertisement drawn for Insel-Verlag, 1924, signed 'IT' in corner. Reduced. The trademark was drawn by Peter Behrens.

Dieses neue Zeichen
von Johannes Tzschichhold in
Leipzig entworfen und von uns
handelsgerichtlich eingetragen,
wollen wir in Zukunft an die
Stelle unseres früheren Verlags-
signets treten lassen. Wir bitten
unseren verehrten Kundenkreis,
hiervon Kenntnis zu nehmen.

Leipzig-Reudnitz, am 1. Januar 1923

Fischer & Wittig

Kunstverlag und
Buchdruckerei

*

Announcement of a new symbol designed for
Fischer & Wittig, 1923. Actual size.

TAMBOUR

A newspaper title, 1924, in a totally new style.

KSIĄŻKI

WYDAWNICTWA

PHILOBIBLON

w WARSZAWIE

TUTAJ DO NABYCIA

JAN CZYCHOLD

Left:
A typographic poster designed for Philobiblon, publisher, in Warsaw, 1924, reduced. Original in black and gold on white card. The text means 'Books from Philobiblon in Warsaw can be had here'. The poster reflects Tschichold's new ideas on design after visiting the Bauhaus Exhibition in 1923.

Catalogue cover for Insel-Verlag, 1926, actual size. Original in black and green.

DIE BÜCHER DES
INSEL=VERLAGS

gehen nicht aus billiger Massen=
fabrikation hervor· Sie erstreben in Papier,
Druck und Einband höchste Leistung· Sie
wollen nicht blenden, sondern dauern·

Insel-Bücherei ⟨der Band 1 M⟩· Vier Mark-Bücher·
Bibliothek der Romane ⟨der Band 5 M⟩· Briefbücher und
Memoiren· Illustrierte und Kunstbücher· Goethe-Bücher·
Deutsche Klassiker auf Dünndruckpapier· Gesamtausgaben
von Balzac, Dickens, Dostojewski, Shakespeare, Tolstoi·
Werke zeitgenössischer Dichter

DIE BÜCHER SIND HIER VORRÄTIG

Advertisement drawn for Insel-Verlag, 1926,
in traditional style. Reduced.

Letterhead in A4 size, 1929.
Carefully designed following standardised
rules.

WERKBUND-AUSSTELLUNG STUTTGART 1929   **film und foto**

Postanschrift des Absenders	Fernruf	Bankkonto:	Postscheckkonto
Werkbund-Ausstellung 1929, Stuttgart, Tagblatt-Turmhaus	24691	Bankhaus Schwarz, Stuttgart	Stuttgart 28441

Ihre Zeichen   Ihre Nachricht vom   Unsere Zeichen   Tag

3

2

Dinformat A4 (210 x 297 mm)   Geschäftsbriefvordruck nach DIN 676   typo tschichold

typographische mitteilungen

zeitschrift des bildungsverbandes der deutschen buchdrucker leipzig ● oktoberheft 1925

sonderheft

elementare typographie

natan altman
otto baumberger
herbert bayer
max burchartz
el lissitzky
ladislaus moholy-nagy
molnár f. farkas
johannes molzahn
kurt schwitters
mart stam
ivan tschichold

Cover, designed by Tschichold, of the Leipzig printing periodical *Typographische Mitteilungen* containing his manifesto 'Elementare Typographie' ('The Principles of Design'). October 1925. Reduced.

ELEMENTARE TYPOGRAPHIE

198

IWAN TSCHICHOLD

1. Die neue Typographie ist zweckbetont.

2. Zweck jeder Typographie ist Mitteilung (deren ??? ??? ?ie darstellt). Die Mitteilung muss in kürzester, einfachster, eindringlichster Form erscheinen.

3. Um Typographie sozialen Zwecken dienstbar zu machen, bedarf es der *inneren* (den Inhalt anordnenden) und *äußeren* (die Mittel der Typographie in Beziehung zueinander setzenden) *Organisation* des verwendeten Materials.

4. *Innere Organisation* ist Beschränkung auf die elementaren Mittel der Typographie: Schrift, Zahlen, Zeichen, Linien des Setzkastens und der Setzmaschine.
Zu den elementaren Mitteln neuer Typographie gehört in der heutigen, auf Optik eingestellten Welt auch das exakte Bild: die Photographie.
Elementare Schriftform ist die **Groteskschrift** aller Variationen: mager — **halbfett** — **fett** — schmal bis **breit**.

Schriften, die bestimmten Stilarten angehören oder beschränkt-nationalen Charakter tragen (**Gotisch**, Fraktur, Kirchenslavisch) sind nicht elementar gestaltet und beschränken zum Teil die internationale Verständigungsmöglichkeit. Die Mediäval-Antiqua ist die der Mehrzahl der heute Lebenden geläufigste Form der Druckschrift. Im (fortlaufenden) Werksatz besitzt sie heute noch, ohne eigentlich elementar gestaltet zu sein, vor vielen Groteskschriften den Vorzug besserer Lesbarkeit.
Solange noch keine, auch im Werksatz gut lesbare elementare Form geschaffen ist, ist zweckmässig eine unpersönliche, sachliche, möglichst wenig aufdringliche Form der Mediäval-Antiqua (also eine solche, in der ein zeitlicher oder persönlicher Charakter möglichst wenig zum Ausdruck kommt) der Grotesk vorzuziehen.

Eine ausserordentliche Ersparnis würde durch die ausschliessliche Verwendung des kleinen Alphabets unter Ausschaltung *aller* Grossbuchstaben erreicht, eine Schreibweise, die von allen Neuerern der Schrift als unsre Zukunftsschrift empfohlen wird. Vgl. das Buch »Sprache und Schrift« von Dr. Porstmann, Beuth-Verlag, G. m. b. H., Berlin SW 19, Beuthstrasse 8. Preis Mark 5.25. — durch kleinschreibung verliert unsre schrift nichts, wird aber leichter lesbar, leichter lernbar, wesentlich wirtschaftlicher. warum für einen laut, z. b. a zwei zeichen A und a? ein laut ein zeichen. warum zwei alfabete für ein wort, warum die doppelte menge zeichen, wenn die hälfte dasselbe erreicht?

typographische mitteilungen

oktoberheft 1925

sonderheft

elementare typographie

zeitschrift des bildungsverbandes der deutschen buchdrucker ● leipzig

mit arbeiten von

natan altman
otto baumberger
herbert bayer
max burchartz
el lissitzky
ladislaus moholy-nagy
molnár f. farkas
johannes molzahn
kurt schwitters
mart stam
ivan tschichold

The last page in *Typographische Mitteilungen*. The two small illustrations show a letterhead and an 'ex-libris', both designed by Tschichold. Reduced.

Links sind drei russische Buchstaben, die im Gedichte erwähnt werden (eR, Scha, Schtscha) abgebildet. Das Auffinden des einzelnen Gedichts wird (*ohne* Inhaltsverzeichnis am Schluß) folgendermaßen bewirkt: Am Rande des Buches sind Fahnen mit Stichwörtern, ähnlich dem A-B-C unsrer Briefordner, durch deren Aufheben man sofort das einzelne Gedicht findet. Durch diese Organisation des Inhalts erreicht Lissitzky zugleich eine bisher unbekannte Plastizität des Buchkörpers, die bei dem geringen Umfang dieses Buches besonders bestidt.

Unter dem Artikel »Elementare Typographie« sind auf den Seiten **198** und **200** zwei ausgezeichnete (verkleinerte) Zeitungsinserate von *Max Burchartz* eingefügt. Die Organisation des Textes und die Schlagkraft des Ganzen sind vorbildlich. Die Abbildung auf Seite **202** ist ein Photoplakat von *Moholy-Nagy,* und zwar eine »Photoplastik«. Eine Photoplastik ist eine Komposition, der Teile von Photographien bildmäßig sinnvoll eingeordnet sind, oder die ganz aus Phototeilen besteht. (Etwas ähnliches ist die »Photomontage«, bei dieser werden ganze Photos zusammengeklebt und komponiert; z.B. wie bei manchen Einbänden des Malikverlags von *John Heartfield* [Jack London]). Die Briefköpfe von *Moholy-Nagy* auf den Seiten **204** und **206** sind ausgezeichnete Leistungen, insbesondere der erste, in dem mit geringsten Mitteln eine überzeugende Wirkung erreicht ist. - Die Abbildung auf Seite **204** unten (einem amerikanischen Inserat unter Weglassung der ungeeigneten Beschriftung entnommen), zum Aufsatz »Die Reklame« gehörig, entstammt einem Flugblatt »Gestaltung der Reklame« von Max Burchartz, Bochum, Bongardstr. 15. Das Bild auf Seite **206** erklärt sich aus dem danebenstehenden Aufsatz. Auf Seite **207** bringen wir einen um weniges verkleinerten Umschlag der ungarischen aktivistischen Zeitschrift MA von *Molnár F. Farkas.* Alkotni – nem alakitani heißt: Schaffen – nicht gestalten! (Gemeint ist, daß an Stelle der zwar nützlichen Versuche endlich reales Schaffen treten soll.) Wie auf vielen neueren aktivistischen Zeitschriften findet sich auf dieser das rote Quadrat, das Sinnbild elementarer Gestaltung. Der Prospekt von *L. Moholy-Nagy,* von dem auf den Seiten **208** und **209** die Innenseiten gezeigt werden, gehört zu den schönsten und gelungensten Beispielen neuer Typographie. Übrigens werden einige der darin angezeigten Bücher bald erscheinen. Dem Leser dieses Heftes, sofern er für die neuen Bestrebungen eintritt, werden insbesondere die Bücher von *El Lissitzky* (22) und *L. Moholy-Nagy* (13) interessieren. Die Postkarte auf Seite **210** oben vom Verfasser ist die im Aufsatz »Elementare

Typographie« erwähnte Arbeit im DINformat A 6 (ab 1. September Postkarten-Weltformat). Die Arbeiten auf den Seiten **210** und **211** sind ohne weiteres verständlich. Eine gute einfarbige Postkarte von *Johannes Molzahn* und ein Typosignet für einen Glasmaler von *Herbert Bayer,* die Abstraktion eines Glasfensters finden sich auf Seite **212**. Der Briefkopf Nina Chmelowa (auf Seite **214**) von *Iwan Tschichold* ist in der oberen rechten Ecke eines Quartbriefs zu denken. Die beherrschende Form des Exlibris am Fuße dieser Seite sind die Anfangsbuchstaben des Namens: I T. Zu den abgebildeten Briefen muß grundsätzlich bemerkt werden, daß man von jetzt an solche nur im DINformat A 4 herstellen und ihnen DINorm 676 zugrundelegen sollte. Nur durch die Befolgung dieser elementaren Regeln kann das heutige Format-Chaos, das sich nicht zum wenigsten auch im Briefwesen bemerkbar macht, beseitigt werden. Wir freuen uns, auf Seite **205** ein außerordentlich schönes Beispiel eines Briefbogens, den von *El Lissitzky* selbst, bringen zu können. Der rote Pfeil zeigt auf das Wörtchen »el«, mit dem Lissitzky seine Arbeiten signiert. (Von Lissitzky stammt übrigens auch der Einband zu Tairoffs »Entfesseltem Theater«, Verlag Kiepenheuer.) Der unterzeichnete Verfasser richtet an alle Freunde neuer Typographie die Bitte, hier nicht gezeigtes und neu entstandenes, in Frage kommendes Material (möglichst in 2 Exemplaren) ihm zuzuschicken. Er beabsichtigt eine größere Ausstellung von Werken neuer Typographie in Leipzig und weitere Fachaufsätze und Vorträge.

Leipzig, im August 1925.   *Iwan Tschichold.*

Am Kopf der Seite: Iwan Tschichold 1924: Briefkopf

Iwan Tschichold 1925: Exlibris

214

Die Bearbeitung und typographische Gestaltung dieses Heftes besorgte Iwan Tschichold, Leipzig. Die »T. M.« erscheinen jeden Monat. Der Postbezugspreis beträgt vierteljährlich 3 Mark. Bei Zustellung unter Kreuzband kostet jedes Heft 1 Mark, ausschließlich Porto. Zuschriften sind an die Geschäftstelle, Leipzig, Salomonstr. 8, zu richten. Herausgeber: Bruno Dreßler; Schriftleiter: Josef Schuster; Inserate: Otto Schröder. Gedruckt in der Buchdruckwerkstätte, G. m. b. H., sämtlich in Leipzig.

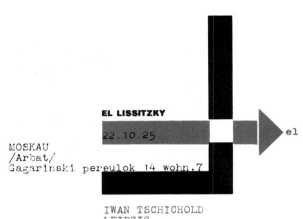

EL LISSITZKY

22.10.25   el

MOSKAU
/Arbat/
Gagarinski pereulok 14 wohn.7

IWAN TSCHICHOLD
LEIPZIG

LIEBER TSCHICHOLD,
              BRAVO,
                  BRAVO,   ich gratuliere Sie herzlichst
mit'der schöner Druckschrift elementare typographie. Es ist
bei mir ein physischer Genuss wenn ich so eine Qualitetsch-
rift in den Händen, Fingern, Augen halte. Meine Nervenante-
nen spannen sich und der gesamte Motor verschneller den Lauf.
Und darauf kommt es schlieslich doch an--die Trägheit zu über-
winden.
Es ist gut und gibt der Sache ihren Wert das die literarische
Hälfte so eincheitlich aufgestellt ist und ohne gewolte Popu-
lertcheit algemeiverständlich ist. Das ist Ihr guter Verdienst.
Es ist ein Erfolg das es ist ein Heft einer Fachzetschrift
/keine Kunstzeitschrift/ und darum hoffe ich wird es erreichen
den werktätigen Drucker und er wird kriegen seinSelbstbewusst-
sein und das wird in anregen zu Erfindungen mit seinem Setzkasten.
Mich persönlich hat das Heft gefreut den es ist eine Bilanz einer
Periode die schon hinter mir ist und die ich heute von der Ferne
betrachten kann. Ich bin jetzt mit Architektur ganz schwanger.
Aber typofragen beschäftigen mich ständig nur hiesige technische
Mittel sind so jämerlich das es ist unmöglich etwas praktisches
/ausser Laborotoriumsarbeit/ zu realisieren. Ein Buch der schon
längst bei mir mit einem amerikanischen Dichter entstanden ist
liegt bis heute in Skizzen den dazu brauche ich eine gute Druckerei, eine gute Photomechanische Anstallt und ein Verläger der
riskieren will. Und die Hauptsache--selbst bei allen Apparaten
und Maschienen stehen. Überhaupt, es ist heute unmöglich alle
Aufgaben die vor uns stehen allein zu bewältigen. Es tut Not
eine Arbeitsgemeinschaft. Aber zu viel subjektivistische Hefe
sitzt noch in uns, denn alle Versuche scheteren.

Ich habe von Max Burchardtz diese Tage eine sehr gute Drucksache
/Stahlgissereiprospekt/ erhalten. Er schrieb mir das Sie bei Ihn
waren. Es ist schön das Ihr zusammengekommen seit. Max ist auf
einem guten Wege. Die Bewegung die wir angefangen haben bringt

Parts of a letter, in actual size, written by El Lissitzky to Tschichold. The opening sentence of the letter 'BRAVO, BRAVO' congratulates Tschichold warmly and affectionately on 'Elementare Typographie'. Note that in this case Lissitzky's address cannot be incorporated in the letterhead design, as it is on p.36.

gute Fruchte.
Sie haben mir mal geschrieben das Sie eine Heft der DAME
senden, aber das habe ich nicht erchalten.
Was ist es für ein Buch Sprache und Schrift /Porstmann/?
Wenn das gut ist können Sie es mir besorgen, ich werde so-
fort Geld überweisen.
Was gibt sonst bei Ihnen schönes? Sie verfolgen sicher die
Fachliteratur, wenn etwas interessantes über Typo erscheint
senden Sie bitte gelegentlich.

Ich wünsche Ihnen viel Gelegencheit neue gute Druckgegen-
stände zu produtiren und drücke Ihre Hand

mit herzlichen Gruss

A letter from El Lissitzky reproduced in *Typographische Mitteilungen*, with the addressee, and the date, incorporated into Lissitzky's design. Reduced.

EL LISSITZKY
6.3.1925
Brione/Locarno
Villino Raetia

Es wäre zum mindesten unproduktiver Zeitverlust, wenn man heute beweisen wollte, dass man nicht mit eigenem Blut und einer Gänsefeder zu schreiben braucht, wenn die Schreibmaschine existiert. Heute zu beweisen, dass die Aufgabe jedes Schaffens, so auch der Kunst, nicht DAR stellen, sondern DA stellen ist, ist ebenfalls unproduktiver Zeitverlust. (Merz)

205

One of a series of film posters designed by
Tschichold for the Phoebus-Palast, Munich,
1927. Reduced.

Film posters for the Phoebus-Palast, Munich, 1927. Reduced.

Film poster for the Phoebus-Palast, Munich, reduced. Original in sepia brown and grey.

JAN TSCHICHOLD

DIE NEUE TYPOGRAPHIE

EIN HANDBUCH FÜR ZEITGEMÄSS SCHAFFENDE

BERLIN **1928**

VERLAG DES BILDUNGSVERBANDES DER DEUTSCHEN BUCHDRUCKER

The famous original title page for *Die neue Typographie*, 1928, reduced.

Beziehungen nachzuweisen und seine Konsequenzen darzulegen, Klarheit über die Elemente der Typographie und die Forderung zeitgemäßer typographischer Gestaltung zu schaffen, ist Gegenstand dieses Buchs. Der Zusammenhang der Typographie mit allen anderen Gestaltungsgebieten, vor allem der Architektur, hat in allen bedeutenden Zeiten bestanden. Heute erleben wir die Geburt einer neuen, großartigen Baukunst, die unserer Zeit das Gepräge geben wird. Wer einmal die tiefe innere Ähnlichkeit der Typographie mit der Baukunst erkannt und die Neue Architektur ihrem Wesen nach begreifen gelernt hat, für den kann kein Zweifel mehr daran sein, daß die Zukunft der Neuen und nicht der alten Typographie gehören wird.

Und es ist unmöglich, daß etwa, wie manche meinen, auch in Zukunft beide Typographien wie noch heute weiter nebeneinander bestehen. Der kommende große Stil wäre keiner, wenn neben der zeitgemäßen noch die Renaissanceform auf irgendwelchen Gebieten, sei es Buchdruck oder Architektur, weiter existierte. Der Romantismus der vergehenden Generation, so verständlich er ist, hat noch nie einen neuen Stil verhindert. So wie es heute absurd ist, Villen wie Rokokoschlösser oder wie gotische Burgen zu bauen wie vor vierzig Jahren, wird man morgen diejenigen belächeln, die die alte Typographie noch weiter zu erhalten trachten.

In dem Kampfe zwischen dem Alten und dem Neuen handelt es sich nicht um die Erschaffung einer neuen Form um ihrer selbst willen. Aber die neuen Bedürfnisse und Inhalte schaffen sich selbst eine auch äußerlich veränderte Gestalt. Und so wenig man diese neuen Bedürfnisse hinwegdisputieren kann, so wenig ist es möglich, die Notwendigkeit einer wirklich zeitgemäßen Typographie zu bestreiten.

Darum hat der Buchdrucker heute die Pflicht, sich um diese Fragen zu bemühen. Einige sind mit Energie und Elan schöpferisch vorangegangen. für die anderen aber gilt es noch fast

ALLES !
zu tun ●

DIE ALTE TYPOGRAPHIE (1450—1914)

Während die Geschichte der Typographie von der Erfindung bis etwa zur Mitte des vorigen Jahrhunderts eine fortlaufende, ruhige Entwicklungskurve zeigt, bietet die Entwicklung seit dieser Zeit das Bild ruckweiser, unorganischer Störungen, einander durchkreuzender Bewegungen, die Tatsachen neuer technischer Erfindungen, die auf die Entwicklung bestimmend einwirken.

Die Typographie der ersten Epoche (1440—1850) beschränkt sich fast ausschließlich auf das Buch. Die Gestaltung der daneben auftauchenden Flugzettel und der wenigen Zeitungen entspricht der der Buchseite. Bestimmendes Element, besonders seit dem Anfang des 16. Jahrhunderts, ist die Type. Die übrigen Teile des Buches erscheinen sekundär, sie sind angefügt, schmückend, nicht Wesensbestandteil. Die Buchgestalt als Ganzes wird im Laufe der Jahrhunderte zwar variiert, aber nicht entscheidend gewandelt. Gutenberg, der nichts anderes im Sinne hatte, als die damalige Buchform — die Handschrift — zu imitieren, entwickelte seine Typen aus der damaligen Buchschrift, der gotischen Minuskel. Sie, die man heute gern religiösen und anderen feierlichen Inhalten vorbehält, diente zu ihrer Zeit zur Niederschrift oder zum Druck aller vorkommenden, auch profaner, Texte. Der Erfinder wählte mit der gotischen Minuskel, der „Textur", eine Schrift zum Vorbild, die für Inhalte von Bedeutung, d. h. für solche Bücher verwendet wurde, deren Inhalt den Horizont nur aktuellen Interesses überschritt. Neben dieser gotischen Minuskel war im täglichen Leben für aktuelle Schriften, Urkunden und kurze Niederschriften die gotische Kursive (in Frankreich Bâtarde genannt) in Gebrauch, die später Schoeffer zur Ausgangsform der von ihm zuerst benutzten Schwabacher machte. Mit diesen zwei Schriftarbeiten begnügte sich das Zeitalter zwischen der Erfindung und dem Beginn des 16. Jahrhunderts. Von den Variationen der Gotisch und der Schwabacher, die mit den Schriften Gutenbergs und Schoeffers die allgemeine Linienführung gemein haben, dürfen wir bei dieser historischen Betrachtung ebenso absehen, wie von den Formen der Antiquatype vor 1500.

Die Buchform als Ganzes gleicht zu dieser Zeit fast vollkommen der Form des geschriebenen spätgotischen Kodex. Sein Reichtum an bemalten, goldgehöhten großen und farbigen kleinen Initialen, die Rubrikatur, die Randleisten der Anfangsseiten werden in das gedruckte Buch übernommen. Ursprünglich mit der Hand eingefügt, werden diese schmückenden Teile bald in Holz geschnitten und mit gedruckt, bei kostbareren Ausführungen eines Buches nachträglich koloriert. Der Satz in zwei Kolumnen überwiegt. Die Titel zeigen eine asymmetrische, von Logik nicht übermäßig belastete Aufteilung. Selten, daß axiale Gliederungen erscheinen — sie bleiben auf Italien beschränkt. Die Harmonie von Text, Initialen und Titelei wird von

Double spread from *Die neue Typographie*, reduced. The last sentence on p.14 reads in English: 'That is why printers today have a duty to concern themselves with these questions. Some have forged ahead with energy and creative success: for the rest, however, it seems that there is still almost EVERYTHING to do!'

Business card for Tschichold's wife Edith, 1927.

edith tschichold

planegg bei münchen hofmarckstrasse 39

Advertisement designed by Tschichold, 1932.
Note the careful alignments.

Paul Graupe **Berlin W 9**   Bellevuestrasse 7

Am 17. und 18. Oktober 1932 :   **Auktion 105**

Bücher des 15. bis 20. Jahrhunderts	Die grafische Sammlung Rudolf Tewes	Sammlung Paul Ephraim, Berlin
Inkunabeln	Französische Meister	Gemälde
Holzschnittbücher	des 19. und 20. Jahrhunderts:	Handzeichnungen
Erstausgaben	Daumier, Degas, Manet,	neuerer deutscher Meister
Luxus- und Pressendrucke	Picasso, Renoir	
Kunstliteratur	Eine umfassende	
	Toulouse-Lautrec-Sammlung	

Illustrierter Katalog auf Wunsch

Book jacket for the
novel *Mensch unterm
Hammer* ('Men under
the Hammer'), 1931.

Lenhard: Mensch unterm Hammer

Mensch unterm Hammer

Roman von Josef Lenhard

Die sonderbare Geschichte des sonderbaren Proleten Kilian Narr aus der katholischen bayerischen Pfalz. Unbändiger Freiheits- und Wissensdrang bringt ihn unaufhörlich in Widerstreit mit allen möglichen Obrigkeiten. Dieser Kilian Narr ist zur guten Hälfte Josef Lenhard selbst, der in diesen seinem Erstlingsroman voll bittern Humors Gericht über sich selbst hält.   In Ganzleinen 4.30 RM

Cover of *Typografische Entwurfstechnik*,
showing the five 'A' sizes of paper.
Reduced. Original printed in black on
yellow paper.

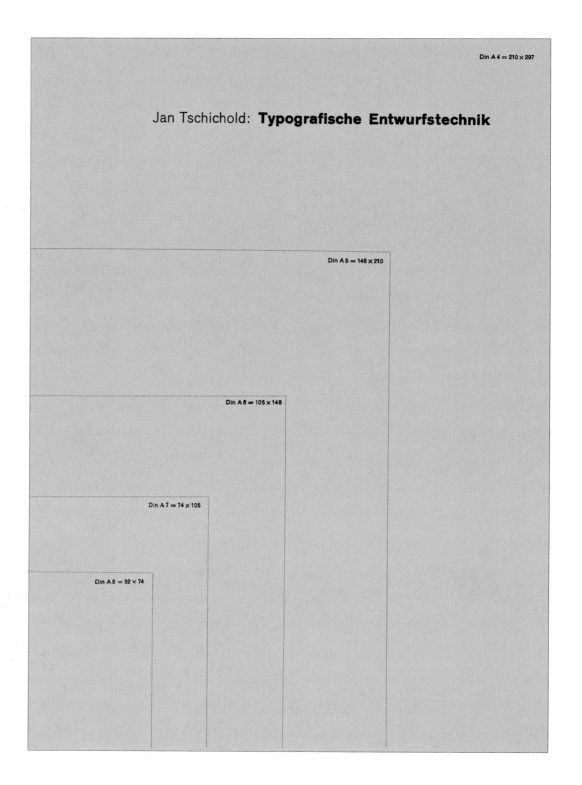

Page 13 of *Typografische Entwurfstechnik*, showing, above, three lines set in 20 point Garamond and five lines in 12 point, and, below, the same type drawn in pencil for a layout.

Garamond mit Kursiv . Schriftgießerei D. Stempel AG, Frankfurt am Main

20 Punkte

Der große Irrtum *unserer Zeit* beruht nun darauf, daß viele meinen GOLDSCHMIEDEKUNST

12 Punkte

Ergreifender noch als diese mehr passiv erlittenen Schicksale sind die Kämpfe derjenigen, die *mit aller Kraft versuchen*, sich allen Widerständen zum Trotz durchzusetzen. Da ist der Sohn eines stellungslosen Ingenieurs, der als Aushilfsschreiber NEUE FRANZÖSISCHE KUNST IN LONDON

Der große Irrtum *unserer Zeit* beruht nun darauf, daß viele meinen GOLDSCHMIEDEKUNST Ergreifender noch als diese mehr passiv erlittenen Schicksale sind die Kämpfe derjenigen, die *mit aller Kraft versuchen*, sich allen Widerständen zum Trotz durchzusetzen. Da ist der Sohn eines stellungslosen Ingenieurs, der als Aushilfsschreiber NEUE FRANZÖSISCHE KUNST IN LONDON

Figurenverzeichnis (12 Punkte)

abcdefghijklmnopqrstuvwxyzäöüchckfffiflftffifflstß&
ABCDEFGHIJKLMNOPQQURSTUVWXYZÄÖÜÆŒ
abcdefghijklmnopqrstuvwxyzäöüchckllffffffffffffflstssttEcr
ABCDEFGHIJKLMNOPQRSTUVWXYZÄÖÜQuQU
*ABCDEGJMNPQuRTÆŒm.n.tz.,-:;!?)([†S',,»«**
1234567890 - 1234567890 - *1234567890 - 1234567890*

der Mediäval klar erscheinen. In den kleinern Graden ist dies ohnehin schwer zu erreichen. Selbstverständlich ist es besser, wenn größere skizzierte Grade schon zeigen, daß eine Mediäval gemeint ist.
Wir setzen also (etwa mit dem Stift Nr. 2) die Buchstaben aus einzelnen Strichen, ähnlich wie die halbfette Grotesk, zusammen, wobei wir darauf achten, daß die Striche senkrecht betont sind. Es kommt nicht darauf an, daß jeder Buchstabe seine sämtlichen Schraffen erhält. Andeutungen genügen. Neu ist hier die Kursiv, eine schräge, enge, aus der Handschrift abgeleitete Type, die als Auszeichnung verwendet wird.

6 Punkte

Da das Leben *Wilhelm Raabes* durch die unermüdliche Arbeit seiner Freunde erforscht ist
AUSZUG AUS DER RAABE-FESTSCHRIFT

7 Punkte

Anthologien können eine künstlerische Idee, ein kulturelles Thema oder die bloße, sehr
SOCIETÄTS-VERLAG FRANKFURT-M

8 Punkte

In der Kleinoktavausgabe von *Siegmund Freuds* Schriften sind jetzt erschienen
SCHICKSAL EINER OBERPRIMA

9 Punkte

Siebzehn *junge Menschen* in feierlich dunklem Anzug stehen auf
GYMNASTIK-UNTERRICHT

10 Punkte

Die Bilanz der *Werftindustrie* für das vergangene Jahr zeigt

14 Punkte

Auf einer Hebrideninsel westlich Schottlands

16 Punkte

Der *bedeutende* Faktor ist die Beleuchtung

20 Punkte

Kurzstreckenlauf

24 Punkte

Domrestaurant

36 Punkte

Inkunabel

48 Punkte

Einkauf

60 Punkte

Nadel

72 Punkte

Herd

Page 15 of *Typografische Entwurfstechnik* showing type in 'black letter' (Fraktur) and as drawn for a layout.

20 Punkte

Pariser Jagdausstellung
Scheibenschießen
HUBERTUS *TREIBER*

8 Punkte

Die Begriffe körperlicher Schönheit sind stark verwirrt. Die Formen des menschlichen Körpers, der den schönheitlichen Höhepunkt der menschlichen Schöpfung repräsentieren soll, *sind dem größten Teil der Menschheit fremd*
DR. STEINTEL: *KÖRPERKULTUR EINST UND JETZT*

Pariser Jagdausstellung
Scheibenschießen
HUBERTUS *TREIBER*

Die Begriffe körperlicher Schönheit sind stark verwirrt. Die Formen des menschlichen Körpers, der den schönheitlichen Höhepunkt der menschlichen Schöpfung repräsentieren soll, *sind dem größten Teil der Menschheit fremd*
DR. STEINTEL: *KÖRPERKULTUR EINST UND JETZT*

Figurenverzeichnis (8 Punkte)

abcdefghijklmnopqrstuvwxyzffffiflßäöü& 1234567890
ABCDEFGHIJKLMNOPQRSTUVWXYZ
abcdefghijklmnopqrstuvwxyzffffiflßäöü& 1234567890
ABCDEFGHIJKLMNOPQRSTUVWXYZ

Die **fette Antiqua,** der Art nach zur französischen Antiqua gehörig, zeigt sehr fette Grundstriche, jedoch Schraffen in der Stärke des Normalschnitts. Sie ist viel fetter als man erst meint. Selbst die kleinsten Grade wirken schon sehr auffällig. Man muß sie also mit Vorsicht verwenden, eher kleinere als größere Grade nehmen. Die fette Antiqua ist eine gute, modern wirkende Auszeichnungsschrift. Man sieht sie aber auch zuweilen als Grundschrift. Von großer Eigenart ist auch ihre Kursiv, die zu Unrecht in Vergessenheit geraten ist. Diese kann auch als selbständige Schrift in Hauptzeilen Verwendung finden. Bei Mischungen mit normaler Antiqua in der Zeile muß man darauf achten, daß die Höhen der Bilder des n möglichst übereinstimmen. Gegebenenfalls muß man den Grad wechseln.
Wir studieren diese Schrift im Sinne unserer früheren Übungen.

5 Punkte
B. Traven : Die Brücke im Dschungel
MODERNE *FRAUEN-ROMANE*

6 Punkte
Weinbrand-Extraangebot *Fl. 5.75*
„SILESIA" HAUSMARKE

7 Punkte
Internationales Tennisturnier
BUDAPEST-BERLIN

7 Punkte gr. Bild (8 Punkte nebenan)
Nordlandreisen Herbst 1932
HAPAG-SEEDIENST

9 Punkte
Goldstandard und Börse
BETRACHTUNGEN

10 Punkte
Der elegante *Ballschuh*
TYP „ERIKA"

12 Punkte
Hamburg von *heute*
LEO-HEIMFILM

14 Punkte
Rundfunk-*Rede*

16 Punkte
Erfinder*geist*

28 Punkte (20 Punkte nebenan)
Manfred

32 Punkte
Kunde

40 Punkte
Zeche

48 Punkte
Bund

60 Punkte
Hut

Ferner lieferbar in den Graden 72 und 84 Punkte

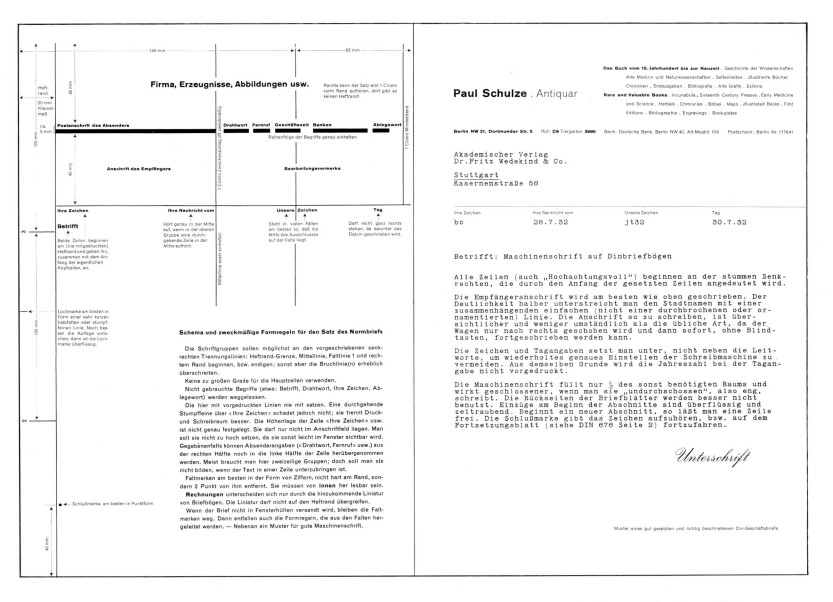

Double spread from *Typografische Entwurfstechnik* demonstrating the grid on which a business letterhead should be designed. Reduced.

Invitation notice for
a lantern lecture by
Tschichold (entrance
free) in 1927.
Reduced.

jan tschichold:

lichtbildervortrag die neue typographie

am mittwoch, 11. mai 1927, abends 8 uhr, in der aula der graphischen berufsschule,
pranckhstraße 2, am marsfeld, straßenbahnlinien: 3 (haltestelle hackerbrücke),
1, 4 und 11 (haltestelle pappenheimstraße) ● der vortrag wird von über hundert
größtenteils mehrfarbigen lichtbildern begleitet, eine diskussion findet nicht statt

freier eintritt

**veranstalter:
bildungsverband
der deutschen
buchdrucker
ortsgruppe
münchen
vorsitzender:
j. lehnacker
münchen
fröttmaninger·
straße 14 c**

Le Capital
FONDERIE

SASKIA

frohe Farben in das sonnige Bild des Sommers

zu tragen, und alle modischen Pastelltöne

finden die anderen, die für ihre Erscheinung

eine ruhigere Note lieben. Kurz- oder lang-

ärmelige Jäckchen werden zu diesen duftigen

Two typefaces designed by Tschichold: above, Transito, for Amsterdam Typefoundry, 1931; below, Saskia, for Schelter & Giesecke, Leipzig, 1931.

Jan Tschichold:

Typographische Gestaltung

Benno Schwabe & Co . Basel 1935

Title page for *Typographische Gestaltung* ('Typographic Design'), 1935, actual size. Note the (at the time) highly unconventional mixture of typefaces. An English translation of this important book, partially re-edited by Tschichold, was published in 1967 under the title of *Asymmetric Typography*.

Jacket of the Dutch edition of *Typographische Gestaltung*, Amsterdam, 1935, actual size. Original in black and green on yellow paper.

Dit boek wil een nieuw typografisch inzicht ingang doen vinden

Typografische vormgeving

Jan Tschichold

● Een nieuwe typografische traditie is de wensch van vele boekdrukkers. Natuurlijk eischen de groote veranderingen in de zet- en druktechniek van de laatste jaren een aangepaste typografische vormgeving. Hierover en over de noodzakelijk-heid verantwoord te werken, zooals de oude boekdrukkers, handelt dit boek. De schrijver heeft de vormgeving in den nieuwen typografischen stijl gedurende een reeks van jaren reeds overwegend beïnvloed.

MICHELET

UND

DEUTSCHLAND

=

Werner Kaegi

Book cover for Benno Schwabe, 1935,
on toned paper, actual size.

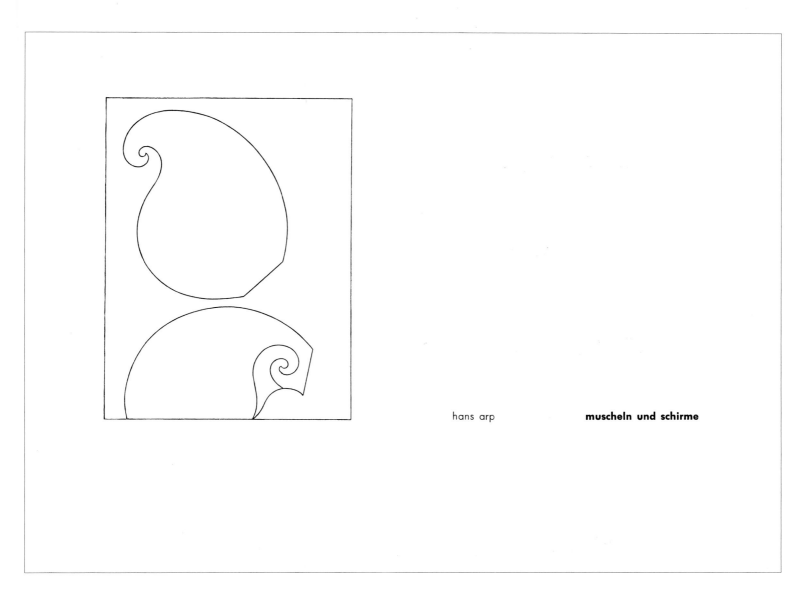

hans arp   **muscheln und schirme**

Title page opening for a book of poems by
Tschichold's friend Hans Arp, 1939.
The drawing is by Sophie Taeuber-Arp.

Percy Lund Humphries & Co Ltd · The Country Press Bradford

Printers
Publishers
Binders

London Office: 12 Bedford Square, w.c.1
Telephone: Museum 7676
Telegrams: Lund Museum 7676 London

Bradford: Telephone 3408 (two lines)
Telegrams: Typography Bradford

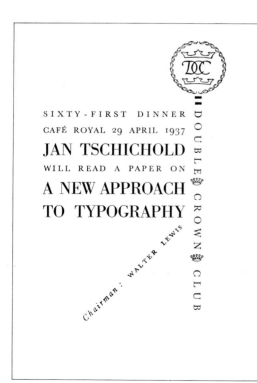

When Jan Tschichold was invited to talk to
the Double Crown Club in London in 1937,
he was not asked to design the menu.
The design used sadly shows how little
Tschichold's ideas, and those of the modern
movement generally, were understood in
England at that time. Reduced: original was
printed in black, red, blue and gold on
cream paper.

Letterhead in the 'new typography' for the
Bradford printers Lund Humphries, 1935.

philobiblon

eine zeitschrift für bücherliebhaber . a magazine for book-collectors

herbert reichner verlag, wien VI (vienna), strohmayergasse 6

telephon	b 23854
bankkonto	wiener bankverein, wien XIV
postscheckkonten	leipzig 8442
	wien 46469
	prag 501701
	zürich VII 18122

Letterhead for *Philobiblon*, a magazine
published in Vienna, before 1940.

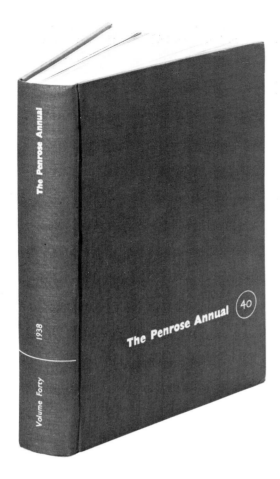

The Penrose Annual

Review of the Graphic Arts   *Edited by* R. B. Fishenden, *M.Sc.* (*Tech.*), F.R.P.S.

Volume Forty | 1938

LUND HUMPHRIES & Co. LTD.   12 Bedford Square, London, W.1

Perhaps the first important book design work given
to Tschichold in England was *The Penrose Annual*
for Lund Humphries, 1938. Here are the binding
(blocked in white on black) and the title page, both
reduced.

K A L E W A L A

ALTFINNISCHE

VOLKS-

UND

HELDENLIEDER

*

AUSGEWÄHLT

UND

EINGELEITET

VON

KARL MEULI

*

VERLAG

BENNO SCHWABE

BASEL

A title page for Benno Schwabe, Basel, 1939, actual size. The subject is old Finnish folk-poetry.

Die Erfindung Gutenbergs

Design for a cover, Basel, 1940, reduced.
Original in black on dark green paper.
Title in English: 'Gutenberg's Invention'.

Title page for *Goethe's Letters from Switzerland*, Basel, 1941, actual size.

GOETHES

BRIEFE AUS DER SCHWEIZ

1779

————————————

BASEL

HOLBEIN-VERLAG

1941

Cover for a Swiss book catalogue, 1941.

WILLIAM SHAKESPEARE

✳

Romeo und Julia
Hamlet, Prinz von Dänemark
Othello, der Mohr von Venedig

1943

✳✳✳✳✳✳✳✳✳✳✳✳✳✳✳✳✳✳✳✳

VERLAG BIRKHÄUSER BASEL

HOMERS
ODYSSEE

ÜBERSETZT VON JOHANN HEINRICH VOSS

VERLAG BIRKHÄUSER BASEL

Title page for Birkhäuser, Basel, 1943, actual size.

Bookjacket with a drawing by
Hans Fischer, 1943, actual size.

BIRL · DIE KÜHNE KATZE

Ein Märchen von Alexander M. Frey

Mit Zeichnungen von Hans Fischer

Wilhelm Röpke

DIE GESELLSCHAFTS- KRISIS DER GEGENWART

In diesem seit langem erwarteten
Buch gibt der Genfer Nationalökonom
wesentliche Orientierungen
im Chaos unserer Zeit

EUGEN RENTSCH VERLAG

Bookjacket for Eugen Rentsch
Verlag, 1944, actual size.
Original in black and green on
toned paper.

Bookjacket for Stocker, 1944, actual size.
Original in black and red on toned paper.

WILHELM SCHMIDT

★

Sechs

Bücher

von der Liebe

von der Ehe

von der

Familie

★

STOCKER

O
Baſel
du
holtſelig
Statt

★

Gedichte,

Sprüche

und

Inschriften

aus

Basels

Vergangen-

heit

★

Aus-

gewählt

von

Paul

Koelner

★

Verlag

Birkhäuser

Basel

O Baſel du holtſelig Statt

Gedichte, Sprüche und Inschriften

Bookjacket for Birkhäuser, Basel, 1944, actual size, on toned paper.

ECKERMANNS GESPRÄCHE MIT GOETHE

Vollständige Ausgabe in zwei Bänden
Herausgegeben von Ernst Merian·Genast
Zweiter Band

JOHANN PETER ECKERMANN

GESPRÄCHE MIT GOETHE

IN DEN LETZTEN JAHREN

SEINES LEBENS

—

1823·1832

—

1945

VERLAG BIRKHÄUSER BASEL

Half title and title page for
Birkhäuser, Basel, 1945, actual size.

Die
Feuerschützen-Gesellschaft
zu Basel

★

IM AUFTRAGE DER

GESELLSCHAFT VERFASST VON

PAUL KOELNER

★

1946

VERLAG BIRKHÄUSER · BASEL

Title page for Birkhäuser, Basel, 1946, reduced.

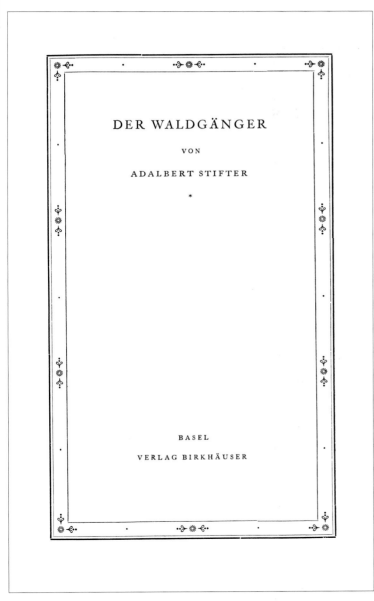

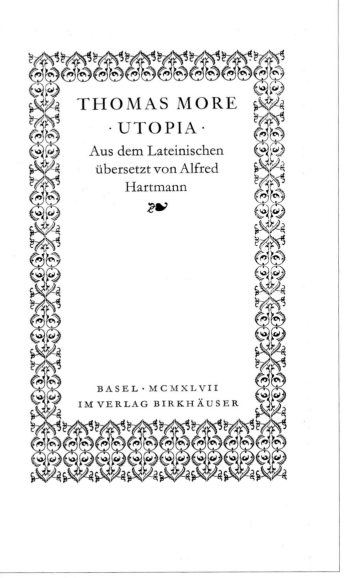

Two title pages for the Birkhäuser Collection, 1944 and 1947.
Tschichold's work from 1941 for Birkhäuser was admired by Oliver
Simon in London and provided proof of his appropriate capabilities
when Allen Lane later asked Simon whom he should ask to redesign
Penguin Books after the war.

HOMERS
WERKE
I
ODYSSEE

—

ÜBERSETZT
VON
JOHANN
HÉINRICH
VOSS

HOMERS ODYSSEE

ÜBERSETZT VON JOH. HEINR. VOSS (1781)
HERAUSGEGEBEN UND EINGELEITET
VON PETER VON DER MÜHLL

Wohl kaum eine andere Dichtung verdient eher durch eine wohlfeile aber würdige Ausgabe weitesten Kreisen zugänglich gemacht zu werden, als das unvergängliche Frühwerk der europäischen Literatur, des Griechen Homer Epos von den Irrfahrten des Odysseus und seiner Heimkehr nach Ithaka. Zu viele noch kennen nicht mehr als den blossen Umriss der alten Fabel, wie ihn der Geschichtsunterricht vermittelt. Ihre ganze Schönheit enthüllt diese wahrhaft wundervolle Dichtung des Altertums indessen nur dem, der sie in gebundener Fassung liest. Johann Heinrich Voss, der Zeitgenosse Goethes, hat ihr die langersehnte deutsche Form verliehen. Seine Hexameter erstrahlen auch heute noch in jugendlicher Frische und sind die gültige Übersetzung des Gebildeten geblieben. Kein schöneres Geschenk für einen jungen Menschen, kein Werk, das auch dem reifen Manne eine grössere geistige Erquickung gewährt.

BIRKHÄUSER-
KLASSIKER

24

VERLAG BIRKHÄUSER BASEL   3 Fr.

HUGO BALL

DIE FLUCHT AUS DER ZEIT

Book jacket lettered by Tschichold, Switzerland, 1944, actual size. Original printed in black and red on ochre paper.

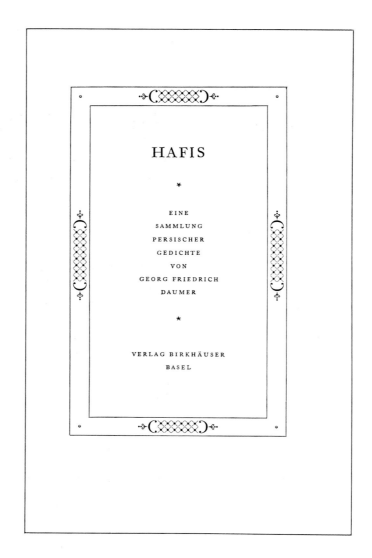

Title page in a style suggested by the subject (Persian poetry),
for Birkhäuser, Basel, 1945, actual size.

SCHATZKAMMER DER SCHREIBKUNST

MEISTERWERKE DER KALLIGRAPHIE AUS VIER JAHRHUNDERTEN

AUSGEWÄHLT UND EINGELEITET VON JAN TSCHICHOLD

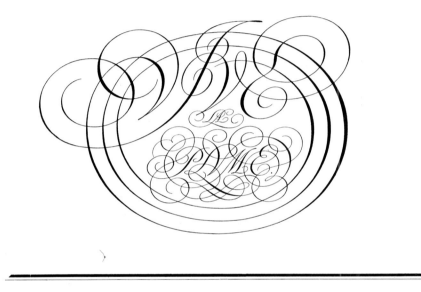

VERLAG BIRKHÄUSER · BASEL

Title page for Tschichold's book on 'Masterworks of calligraphy from four centuries', Birkhäuser, 1945, reduced. An English edition, *Treasury of Alphabets and Lettering*, was published in New York in 1966.

Jacket for Tschichold's book on type and
lettering, second edition, Berlin, 1951, actual
size. The sub-title reads in translation: 'A manual
of type by Jan Tschichold for compositors,
graphic artists, and friends of good type'.
Original in black and red on toned paper.

Schrift

EIN LEHRBUCH DER SCHRIFT

kunde

VON JAN TSCHICHOLD

Schreib

FÜR SETZER

übungen

GRAPHIKER UND FREUNDE

und

GUTER SCHRIFT

Skizzieren

E·R·WEISS SCHRIEB DEM VERFASSER ÜBER DIESES BUCH: SEIEN SIE HERZLICH BEDANKT FÜR DAS NEUE SCHRIFTBUCH · MAN KANN DAS NICHT BESSER MACHEN, IN JEDER BEZIEHUNG ✳ STANLEY MORISON SCHRIEB: LIKE ALL YOUR PUBLICATIONS, YOUR NEW BOOK ON TYPOGRAPHY AND LAYOUT IS MOST PLEASINGLY WRITTEN AND PRINTED · THE BOOK GAINS A GREAT DEAL TOO FROM YOUR OWN CALLIGRAPHY ✳

JAN TSCHICHOLD

Schriftkunde, Schreibübungen und Skizzieren

BERLIN MCMLI

VERLAG DES DRUCKHAUSES

TEMPELHOF

Wenn eine bestimmte Schriftzeile auf einem bestimmten Flächenraum unterzubringen ist, darf nicht in erster Linie nach der größten möglichen Höhe der Buchstaben gesucht werden. Es muß vielmehr ausprobiert werden, welche Größe noch den richtigen Buchstabenabstand erlaubt. Über die richtigen Buchstabenabstände unterrichtet ausführlich der Abschnitt «Grundregeln über Sperren und Ausgleichen» (Seite 83). Ich zeige, was ich meine, an den folgenden drei Beispielen:

1. Ein gegebener Flächenraum, dem das Wort Buchdruckerei in Versalien eingefügt werden soll.

BUCHDRUCKEREI

2. Falsch (unrhythmisch, schwer leserlich). Das Beispiel zeigt die größten, hier möglichen Buchstaben, aber ohne ausreichende Buchstabenzwischenräume. Diese fast überall anzutreffende Art ist sehr mangelhaft.

BUCHDRUCKEREI

3. Richtig (rhythmisch, übersichtlich). Um richtige Buchstabenabstände zu erhalten, die die Schrift erst gut leserlich machen, muß man nämlich eine etwas kleinere Schriftgröße wählen.

85

Häufig ereignet es sich, daß zwei oder mehrere Schriftzeilen untereinander keine großen Längenunterschiede ergeben (Abb. 4). Wenn man den Wortlaut nicht anders brechen kann (womit sich vielleicht ein lebhafterer Umriß ergäbe, Abb. 8), so darf man sich nicht bemühen, durch Auseinanderziehen oder Zusammenpressen der Buchstaben gleiche Zeilenlängen zu erreichen (Abb. 4 und 5). Ebenso unschön ist es, die Buchstaben der einen Zeile breiter oder schmäler als die der andern zu zeichnen, um gleiche Zeilenlängen zu erhalten. Richtig sind nur die Lösungen 6, 7 und 8.

DRUCKEREI
UND VERLAG

4. Falsch.

DRUCKEREI
UND
VERLAG

5. Falsch.

DRUCKEREI
UND VERLAG

· 6. Richtig.

DRUCKEREI
UND VERLAG

7. Richtig.

DRUCKEREI
UND
VERLAG

8. Richtig.

Two pages from *Schriftkunde*, 1951, reduced.
Tschichold's text in translation, p.85:
'When a given line has to be set in a given space, the largest possible size of type should not be chosen. The following three examples show what I mean:
1. A given space in which the word "Buchdruckerei" must be placed in capitals.
2. Wrong (jarring, difficult to read)… The letters are too close together. This mistake is all too common.
3. Right (harmonious, clear). In order to obtain good letter-spacing, a small size of type must be chosen.
p.86: Nos 4 and 5 are wrong, 6, 7 and 8 are right.'

Jan Tschichold at Penguin Books, London, 1948.

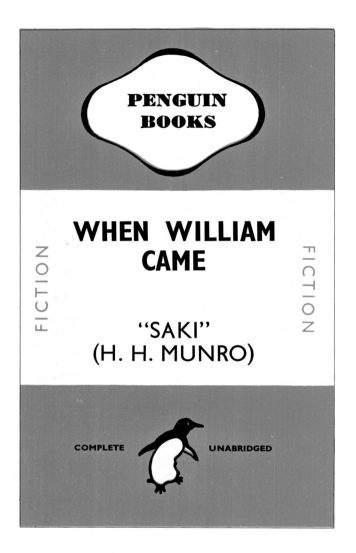

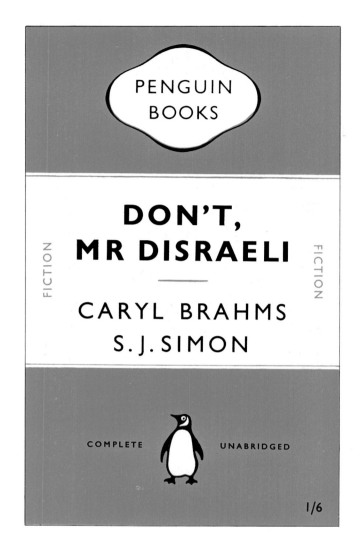

Left: the Penguin paperback cover as Tschichold found it in 1947. This was Penguin no.331, first published in 1941.

Right: Tschichold's refinement of the standard Penguin cover, 1949, with the Penguin symbol redrawn. Both covers reduced.

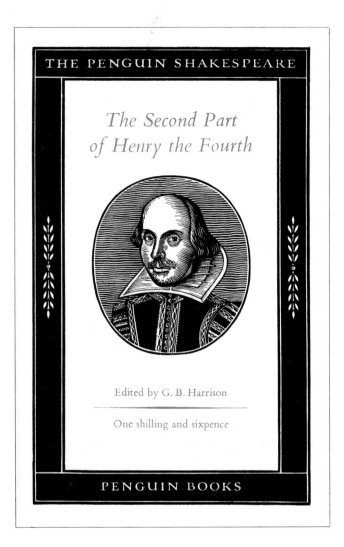

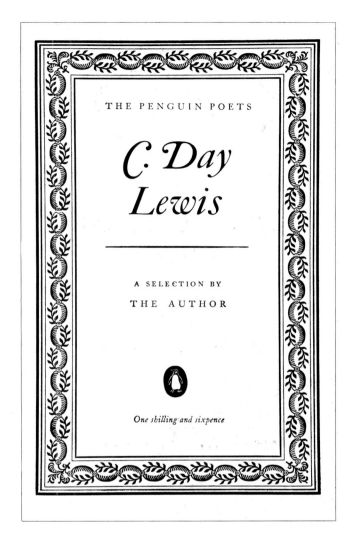

Cover for the Penguin Shakespeare, 1947.
The portrait was engraved on wood by
Reynolds Stone, the typography and lettering
on the borders are by Tschichold. Reduced.

The Penguin Poets series, 1949. The type is all
in black, the rules, border and symbol are
printed in green.

Penguin Composition Rules

All text composition should be as closely word-spaced as possible. As a rule, the spacing should be about a middle space or the thickness of an 'i' in the type size used.

Wide spaces should be strictly avoided. Words may be freely broken whenever necessary to avoid wide spacing, as breaking words is less harmful to the appearance of the page than too much space between words.

All major punctuation marks – full point, colon, and semicolon – should be followed by the same spacing as is used throughout the rest of the line.

INDENTING OF PARAGRAPHS

The indent of the paragraph should be the em of the fount body.

Omit indents in the first line of the first paragraph of any text and at the beginning of a new section that comes under a sub-heading. It is not necessary to set the first word in small capitals, but if this is done for any reason, the word should be letter-spaced in the same way as the running title.

If a chapter is divided into several parts without headings, these parts should be divided not only by an additional space, but always by one or more asterisks of the fount body. As a rule, one asterisk is sufficient. Without them it is impossible to see whether a part ends at the bottom of a page or not. Even when the last line of such a part ends the page, there will always be space for an asterisk in the bottom margin.

PUNCTUATION MARKS AND SPELLING

If this can be done on the keyboard, put thin spaces before question marks, exclamation marks, colons, and semicolons.

Between initials and names, as in G. B. Shaw and after all abbreviations where a full point is used, use a smaller (fixed) space than between the other words in the line.

Instead of em rules without spaces, use en rules preceded and followed by the word space of the line, as in the third paragraph above.

Marks of omission should consist of three full points. These should be set without any spaces, but be preceded and followed by word spaces.

1

Use full points sparingly, and omit after these abbreviations: Mr, Mrs, Messrs, Dr, St, WC2, 8vo, and others containing the last letter of the abbreviated word.

Use single quotes for a first quotation and double quotes for quotations within quotations. If there is still another quotation within the second, return to single quotes. Punctuation belonging to a quotation comes within the quotes, otherwise outside.

Opening quotes should be followed by a hairspace except before A and J. Closing quotes should be preceded by a hairspace except after a comma or a full point. If this cannot be done on the keyboard, omit these hairspaces, but try to get the necessary attachment.

When long extracts are set in small type do not use quotes.

Use parentheses ( ) for explanation and interpolations; brackets [ ] for notes.

For all other queries on spelling, consult the *Rules for Compositors and Readers at the University Press, Oxford,* or Collins's *Authors' and Printers' Dictionary*.

CAPITALS, SMALL CAPITALS, AND ITALICS

Words in capitals must always be letter-spaced. The spacing of the capitals in lines of importance should be very carefully optically equalized. The word spaces in lines either of capitals or small capitals should not exceed an en quad.

All display lines set in the same fount should be given the same spacing throughout the book.

Use small capitals for running headlines and in contents pages. They must always be slightly letter-spaced to make words legible.

Running headlines, unless otherwise stated, should consist of the title of the book on the left-hand page, and the contents of the chapter on the right.

Italics are to be used for emphasis, for foreign words and phrases, and for the titles of books, newspapers, and plays which appear in the text. In such cases the definite article 'The' should be printed in roman, unless it is part of the title itself.

In bibliographical and related matter, as a rule, authors' names should be given in small capitals with capitals, and the titles in italics.

FIGURES

Do not mix old style text composition with modern face figures. Either hanging or ranging figures may be used if they are cut in the fount used for the text.

In text matter, numbers under 100 should be composed in letters. Use figures when the matter consists of a sequence of stated

2

Tschichold's Penguin Composition Rules, 1947, reduced. Still well worth reading carefully.

quantities, particulars of age, &c. In dates use the fewest possible figures, 1946-7, not 1946-1947. Divide by an en rule without spaces.

REFERENCES AND FOOTNOTES

The reference to a footnote may be given by an asterisk of the fount body, if there are only a few footnotes in the book, and not more than one per page. But if there are two or more footnotes per page, use superior fraction figures preceded by a thin space.

Do not use modern face fraction figures in any old style fount. Either hanging or ranging fraction figures may be used provided that they are in harmony with the face used for the text. For books composed in any old face letter, we recommend Monotype Superior Figures F627, to be cast on the size two points below the size of the face used.

Footnotes should be set two points smaller than the text. Indent the first line of these with the same number of points as the paragraphs in the text matter. Use equal leading between all lines of footnotes, use the same leading as in the text matter, and put 1-2 point lead underneath the last line in order to get register with the normal lines.

For the numbering of footnotes use normal figures followed by a full point and an en quad. These figures may run either throughout the chapter, or even through the whole book, according to the special instructions given by the typographer.

FOLIOS

These should, as a rule, be set in the same size and face as the text, and in arabic numerals.

Pagination should begin with the first leaf in the book, but the first folio actually appearing is that on the verso of the first page of the text.

When there is preliminary matter whose extent is unknown at the time of making up the text into pages, it is necessary to use lower-case roman numerals, numbered from the first page of the first sheet. The first actually appearing cannot be definitely stated, but may be on the acknowledgements page, or at latest on the second page of the preface. In this case, the first arabic folio to appear will be '2' on the verso of the first text page.

Folios for any text matter at the end of the book, such as index &c., should continue the arabic numbering of the text pages.

THE PRINTING OF PLAYS

The same rules should apply to the printing of plays as to the printing of prose. Names of characters should be set in capitals

and small capitals. The text following is indented. Stage directions should be in italics, enclosed in square brackets. The headline should include the number of the act and the scene.

THE PRINTING OF POETRY

For printing poetry use type of a smaller size than would be used for prose. All composition should be leaded and the words evenly spaced with middle spaces. The titles should be centred on the measure, not on the first line. The beginning of each poem may be treated as a chapter opening, with small capitals, &c.

Extra leading, especially between verses of irregular length, may often be misleading, as it is impossible to see whether the verse ends at the bottom of the page or not. The safest way of recognizing the poet's intention is to indent the first line of every new verse, after which leading is not really necessary. Therefore, the first line of the second and following verses should be indented, unless the poet has indicated a shape not allowing for indentations.

MAKE-UP

Books should, with certain exceptions, be made up in the following order:

I. Preliminary pages: 1, half title; 2, frontispiece; 3, title; 4, Imprint or date of publication; 5, dedication; 6, acknowledgements; 7, contents; 8, list of illustrations; 9, list of abbreviations; 10, preface; 11, introduction; 12, errata.

II. The text of the book.

III. Additional matter: 1. appendix; 2. author's notes; 3. glossary; 4. bibliography; 5. index.

The above should each begin on a right-hand page, imprint and frontispiece excepted. As a rule, chapter headings should be dropped a few lines.

The preliminary pages should be set in the same face and style as the book itself. Avoid bold faces.

The index should be set in two or more columns and in type two points smaller than the text. The first word of each letter of the alphabet should be set in small capitals with capitals.

Jan Tschichold

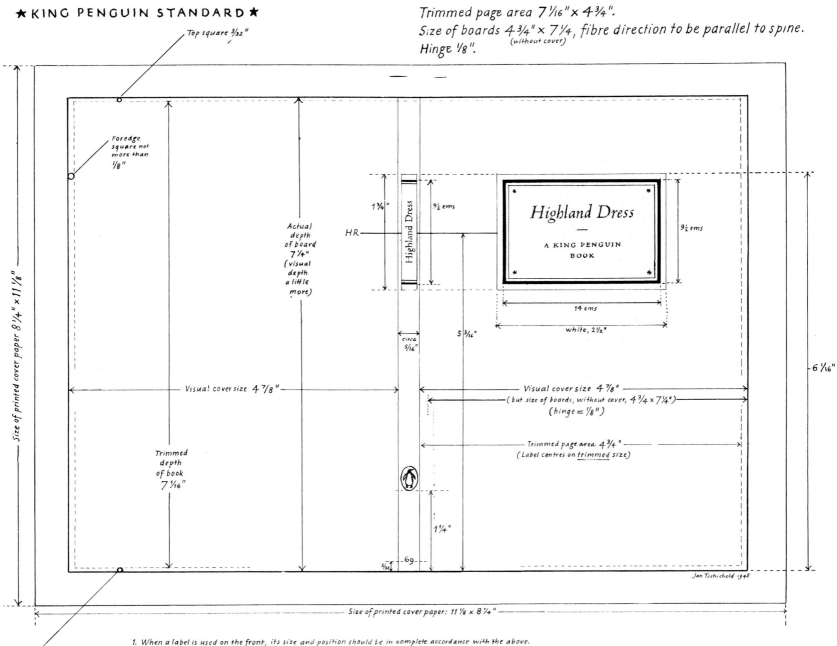

Trimmed page area 7 1/16" x 4 3/4".
Size of boards 4 3/4" x 7 1/4, fibre direction to be parallel to spine.
(without cover)
Hinge 1/8".

Top square 3/32"

Foredge
square not
more than
1/8"

Actual
depth
of board
7 1/4"
(visual
depth
a little
more)

1 3/4"

Highland Dress

9 1/2 ems

HR

Highland Dress

9 1/2 ems

A KING PENGUIN
BOOK

14 ems

white, 2 1/2"

5 3/16"

circa
5/16"

Size of printed cover paper 8 1/4" x 11 1/8"

6 1/16"

Visual cover size 4 7/8"

Visual cover size 4 7/8"
(but size of boards, without cover, 4 3/4 x 7 1/4")
(hinge = 1/8")

Trimmed page area 4 3/4"
(Label centres on *trimmed* size)

Trimmed
depth
of book
7 1/16"

1 1/4"

5/32" 69

Jan Tschichold 1948

Tail square 3/32"

Size of printed cover paper: 11 1/8 x 8 1/4"

1. When a label is used on the front, its size and position should be in complete accordance with the above.
2. The lettering on the labels not to be drawn but in type, in harmony with the type used in the book.
3. Position and style of the spine label, when used, is the same throughout the series, with the thickness altered if necessary, according to the thickness of the book.
4. If there is no label proper on the front, try to avoid a label on the spine and centre lettering to the horizontal rule HR.
5. The position of the King Penguin sign is unalterable. It must appear within a black-bordered oval if there is a label on the spine or its background does not allow for an unbordered sign, but otherwise it should appear without an oval. Good photographs of the design wanted are obtainable from the Penguin Office.
6. The number to appear on the bottom as indicated. Its position is unalterable. Size: 9 pt. No "K".

The 'grid' or standard instructions to printers for King Penguin covers (paper on boards), devised and drawn by Tschichold, 1948, reduced.

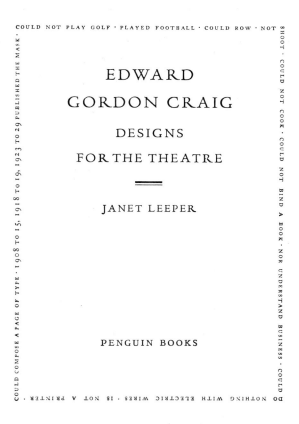

Title page opening for the King Penguin on Edward Gordon Craig, 1948.

PAUL RICHARDS

A BOOK OF MOSSES

→»⟩ ⟨«←

WITH 16 PLATES
FROM JOHANNES HEDWIG'S
DESCRIPTIO MUSCORUM

→»⟩ ⟨«←

PENGUIN BOOKS · LONDON

Misericords

MEDIEVAL LIFE IN ENGLISH WOODCARVING

BY

M. D. ANDERSON

PENGUIN BOOKS

Two contrasting King Penguin title pages, 1950 and 1954. The illustrations in *Mosses* are delicate and linear. The illustrations for *Misericords* are strong black-and-white photographs. The word 'Misericords' and the crown were drawn by Berthold Wolpe.

BRITISH MILITARY UNIFORMS

BY JAMES LAVER

PENGUIN BOOKS

LONDON

Title page and first text page of a King Penguin, 1948, reduced. The illustrations are figures of soldiers reproduced in colour.

THE history of military uniforms is (perhaps fortunately) much shorter than the history of warfare. Men have been fighting in more or less organized bodies since (and perhaps before) they became men. They have worn uniforms, in the proper sense, only for just under three hundred years. It is therefore possible to deal with the subject within the limits of a brief survey, on the condition that the minutiæ of regimental differences are resolutely ignored. The different colours of the facings, the different spacing of the buttons on the uniforms of two separate regiments of foot guards in the second half of the eighteenth century – these are matters which can (and must) be left to specialists, if only for the reason that their adequate discussion would require not one volume but a hundred. In dealing with uniforms there are, in fact, four sets of variables, and even if we confine ourselves to one country there are still three: regiment, period and rank. Even when all these are constant, there may be different uniforms for different purposes: undress, fatigue and the like. Added to this is the frequent difficulty of deciding the exact forms of early uniforms from the inadequacy of the records, the inaccuracies of painters and the eccentricities of individual officers. Local patriotism has sometimes been called in, still further to confuse the issue, as in the bitter controversies which have raged concerning the question of the 'clan tartans' of the Highland regiments. All these matters are outside the scope of the present study, the object of which is merely to record the main lines of evolution, to attempt, in however inadequate a fashion, to penetrate to the reasons why uniforms developed in the way they did

5

THE

ISLE OF WIGHT

——

Illustrated and described
by
BARBARA JONES

Penguin Books

HARMONDSWORTH · MIDDLESEX

A PROSPECT OF

Wales

—

A SERIES OF WATER-COLOURS
BY KENNETH ROWNTREE
AND AN ESSAY BY
GWYN JONES

PENGUIN BOOKS

LONDON

Two King Penguin title pages, 1950 and 1948,
reduced. The illustrations in both books are
strong paintings, reproduced in colour.

WOODCUTS OF
ALBRECHT DÜRER

BY T. D. BARLOW

PENGUIN BOOKS
LONDON

THE art of printing from wood blocks upon fabrics or paper is of great antiquity. It is, however, impossible to say when it was first invented or even to date its introduction into Germany. The fifteenth century saw a rapid development of the woodcut in that country, and the famous Buxheim St Christopher is dated as early as 1423, though it is not certain that this date does actually refer to the year of its execution.

The medium was used for making playing-cards, of which there was a large manufacture at Ulm, and for woodcuts, primitive in design and usually crudely coloured, that were produced for distribution to pilgrims at popular shrines. Somewhat later, or even contemporaneously, followed the block books, though the majority of those which survive are not as early as was formerly supposed. Lastly the woodcut came to be used for book illustration, a development which infinitely increased its scope and potentialities.

Woodcutting in its modern form — the form which should really be called wood engraving — developed at the end of the eighteenth century. The wood engraver works with a graver *against* the grain of the block, which is commonly boxwood. The woodcuts of Dürer's period were produced by a totally different technique. The block consisted of a softer wood, such as pearwood, and was cut with a knife *with* the grain. There is thus no real relationship between the two processes, and even the woods used are of totally different consistency. In Dürer's day the artist drew the design on the block, or it was transferred thereto by a copyist; the block was then cut by a professional woodcutter, or *Formschneider* as he was called. The name of one, Hieronymus Andreä, who cut a number of Dürer's blocks with extreme skill, should especially be mentioned.

5

Title page and first text page of a King Penguin, 1948. Dürer's woodcuts are all reproduced in fine line.

BALLOONING

BY C. H. GIBBS-SMITH

COMPANION ROYAL AERONAUTICAL SOCIETY

WITH THIRTY-TWO PLATES

PENGUIN BOOKS · LONDON

MCMXLVIII

THE KING PENGUIN BOOKS

EDITOR: N. B. L. PEVSNER · TECHNICAL EDITOR: R. B. FISHENDEN

PUBLISHED BY PENGUIN BOOKS LIMITED,

HARMONDSWORTH, MIDDLESEX, ENGLAND

AND BY PENGUIN BOOKS PTY, LTD, 200 NORMANBY ROAD,

MELBOURNE, AUSTRALIA

THIS BOOK
FIRST PUBLISHED
1948

TEXT PAGES PRINTED AT THE CURWEN PRESS, PLAISTOW
COLOUR PLATES MADE BY JOHN SWAIN AND SON, LTD, BARNET, HERTS
AND PRINTED BY BALDING AND MANSELL, WISBECH, CAMBS
COVER DESIGNED BY MARIAN MAHLER
MADE IN GREAT BRITAIN

Title page and verso of a King Penguin, 1948. The intensely dramatic illustrations are mostly in colour, but include black-and-white photographs. Note the care with which even the verso of the title page has been designed. Reduced.

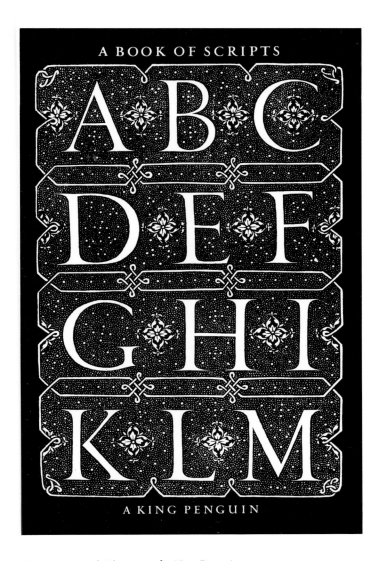

A BOOK OF SCRIPTS

by Alfred Fairbank

Penguin Books

Front cover and title page of a King Penguin, revised edition, 1955, reduced. The cover was adapted by Tschichold from a design by Juan de Yciar of 1547.

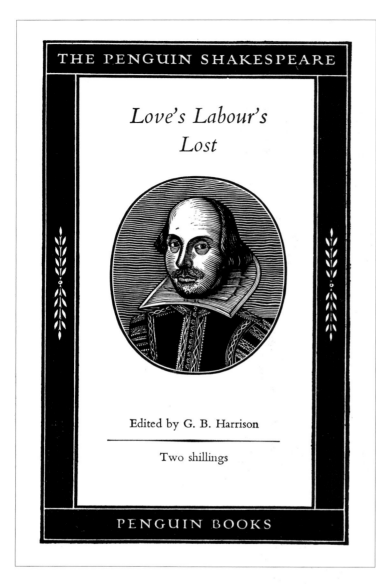

THE PENGUIN SHAKESPEARE

*Love's Labour's
Lost*

Edited by G. B. Harrison

Two shillings

PENGUIN BOOKS

WILLIAM SHAKESPEARE

*Love's Labour's
Lost*

PENGUIN BOOKS
MELBOURNE · LONDON · BALTIMORE

Cover and title page of *Love's Labour's Lost*
in the Penguin Shakespeare series, designed
by Tschichold, 1953, reduced. The portraits
on the cover and title page were engraved
on wood by Reynolds Stone.

Prospectus cover, 1947, with Pelican symbol drawn by Berthold Wolpe. The terracotta second colour on the original gave an extra elegance.

THE

TO BE PUBLISHED BY

PELICAN

PENGUIN BOOKS LIMITED

HISTORY

HARMONDSWORTH · MIDDLESEX

OF ART

The
PENROSE ANNUAL

Edited by R. B. Fishenden M.Sc. (Tech.) F.R.P.S.

VOLUME XLIII

LUND HUMPHRIES & CO. LTD., 12 BEDFORD SQUARE W.C.1

LONDON 1949

THE PENROSE ANNUAL

REVIEW OF THE GRAPHIC ARTS

EDITED BY R. B. FISHENDEN · M.SC. (TECH.) F.R.P.S.

VOLUME FORTY-THREE

1949

PERCY LUND HUMPHRIES & CO · LTD

TWELVE BEDFORD SQUARE

LONDON WC · I

THE COMEDY

OF

DANTE ALIGHIERI

THE FLORENTINE

*

CANTICA I

HELL

⟨L'INFERNO⟩

*

TRANSLATED BY
DOROTHY L. SAYERS

*

PENGUIN BOOKS

Title page of Penguin edition of Dante's *Inferno*, reprinted 1960, actual size. Note the three asterisks to which Dorothy Sayers took objection (see p.12).

Cover of a Puffin Picture book, published by Penguin in 1950, actual size. The title page lettering was drawn by Tschichold, harmonising with the subject and style of the illustrations in the book.

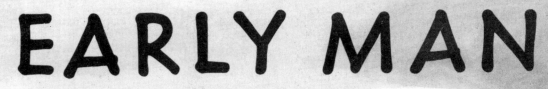

EARLY MAN

Written by Dina Dobson · Illustrated by John Baynes
Puffin Picture Book 87

Two shillings

Another Puffin Picture book, 1950, with title-page lettering in black drawn by Tschichold, in harmony with the style of the illustrations.

AFTER PENGUIN 1950-70

Drawing for Tschichold's Sabon typeface, 1965, actual size. The face was designed for German master printers who required that it should be produced in identical form for both mechanical composition by Linotype and Monotype, and hand composition in foundry types.

Sabon initial.

Sabon Antiqua

ABCDEFGHIJKLMNOPQ
RSTUVWXYZÄÖÜ
abcdefghijklmnopqrstuvwxyz
ßchckffffifflft&äöü
1234567890 1234567890
.,:;-!?.'()[]*†‹›»«„"/£$

In Vorbereitung :

Sabon Kursiv

A full font of Sabon-Antiqua.

RICHARD HÜLSENBECK

DIE NEWYORKER KANTATEN
CANTATES NEW-YORKAISES

MIT SECHS ZEICHNUNGEN VON HANS ARP

AVEC SIX DESSINS DE JEAN ARP

PRÉFACE DE MICHEL SEUPHOR

Cover of booklet of poems in French and German, 1952, slightly reduced. Drawing by Hans Arp. Original printed in black on yellow paper.

I

A Marguerite Hagenbach

Les nuits enroulent leurs voiles
autour des pilotis des ports obscurs.
Nous portons les ténèbres comme on porte un berceau.
Il tombe des étoiles
la poussière glaciale de la tristesse.
Ce n'est ni la tristesse pourtant ni les ténèbres
qui nous enserrent,
mais l'abîme ouvert derrière ténèbres et tristesse:
Cet abîme qui s'empare du dormeur
lorsqu'il sombre en gargouillant dans le rêve sans fin
et dans l'immensité bleue,
à laquelle Dieu, hommes et bêtes ont donné le nom
Cause profonde et chaos   [*d'éternité.*
où tourne le vieil essieu,
roue geignante,
sans cesse poussée par les heures et les jours et les ans,
et pourtant sans lien avec le temps
dans l'espace qui n'est qu'obscurité et pressentiment.
Ainsi nous allons dépariés parmi les autres hommes.
Leur courte pipe à la bouche
ils goûtent le fardeau de chaque jour
plus léger pour eux qui sont de son espèce.
Notre lot est le mal profond
qu'avive en nous le désir d'une liberté plus haute,

8

Opening of the same: the text printed on off-white
paper, with Hans Arp's drawing, slightly reduced, in
black on grey hand-made paper.

JAN TSCHICHOLD

—

Der chinesische und
der japanische mehrfarbige
Holztafeldruck,
technisch

ÜBERREICHT VON
DER PAPIERHANDELSGESELLSCHAFT
BUCHERER, KURRUS & CO · BASEL

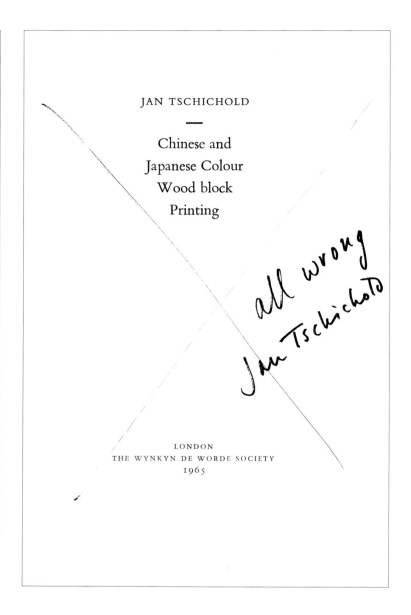

JAN TSCHICHOLD

—

Chinese and
Japanese Colour
Wood block
Printing

all wrong
Jan Tschichold

LONDON
THE WYNKYN DE WORDE SOCIETY
1965

Left: the cover of Tschichold's privately printed booklet on Chinese and Japanese colour printing, 1959, reduced. The Wynkyn de Worde Society in London was given permission to translate and publish it in English, but did not get their edition approved by Tschichold.

Right: the English title page with Tschichold's disapproval written in purple ink.

INHALT

CONTENTS

The two contents pages compared. The typographic differences are minute but significant. Tschichold also objected strongly to the translation: see next pages.

THE ~~BASIC~~ DIFFEREN~~CES~~ ~~OF~~ ^T PROPERTIES (OF
~~BETWEEN~~ CHINESE AND JAPANESE
COLOUR ~~PRINTING~~ PRINTS

THE two varieties of the Far-Eastern polychrome woodcut print, the Chinese and the Japanese, diverge ~~artistically~~ *formally* and technically as much as Chinese and Japanese painting. Although Japanese painting is a descendant of the Chinese model and therefore shares many of its ideas and rules, the accomplished painting reveals here as there the attitude to [particular] each culture. The uninitiated at first see what is obviously common to both of them, thus for many people Chinese and Japanese art, Chinese and Japanese colour prints seem more or less the same and are often ~~easily~~ confused.

No mention of Chinese colour prints is made in Europe before 1907 while Japanese prints have been known in the West since 1862 and have been collected enthusiastically since that time. Hence, good and reliable explanations of the Japanese technique are available. The technique of the Chinese colour print, however, remained obscure until, in 1953, the author of this ~~small book~~ *article* succeeded in unveiling, for the first time, the most important secret of the Chinese colour printing technique, the Registering of Subsequent Colours.

A Chinese colour print is invariably the rendering of an ink or watercolour painting. Although it possesses all the charms of what we call an artist's proof, it is no such thing. The Chinese woodcutter, a highly skilled worker, is no artist. He has to follow the painting slavishly in the most accurate manner. The~~se~~ Chinese paintings normally consist of colour brush strokes ~~of varying size~~ without dark linear contours. At most, the veins of a leaf may be rendered in

7

small or larger

of, for instance, the Ten Bamboo Hall or after a painting of Ch'i Pai-shih,

models,

has said above

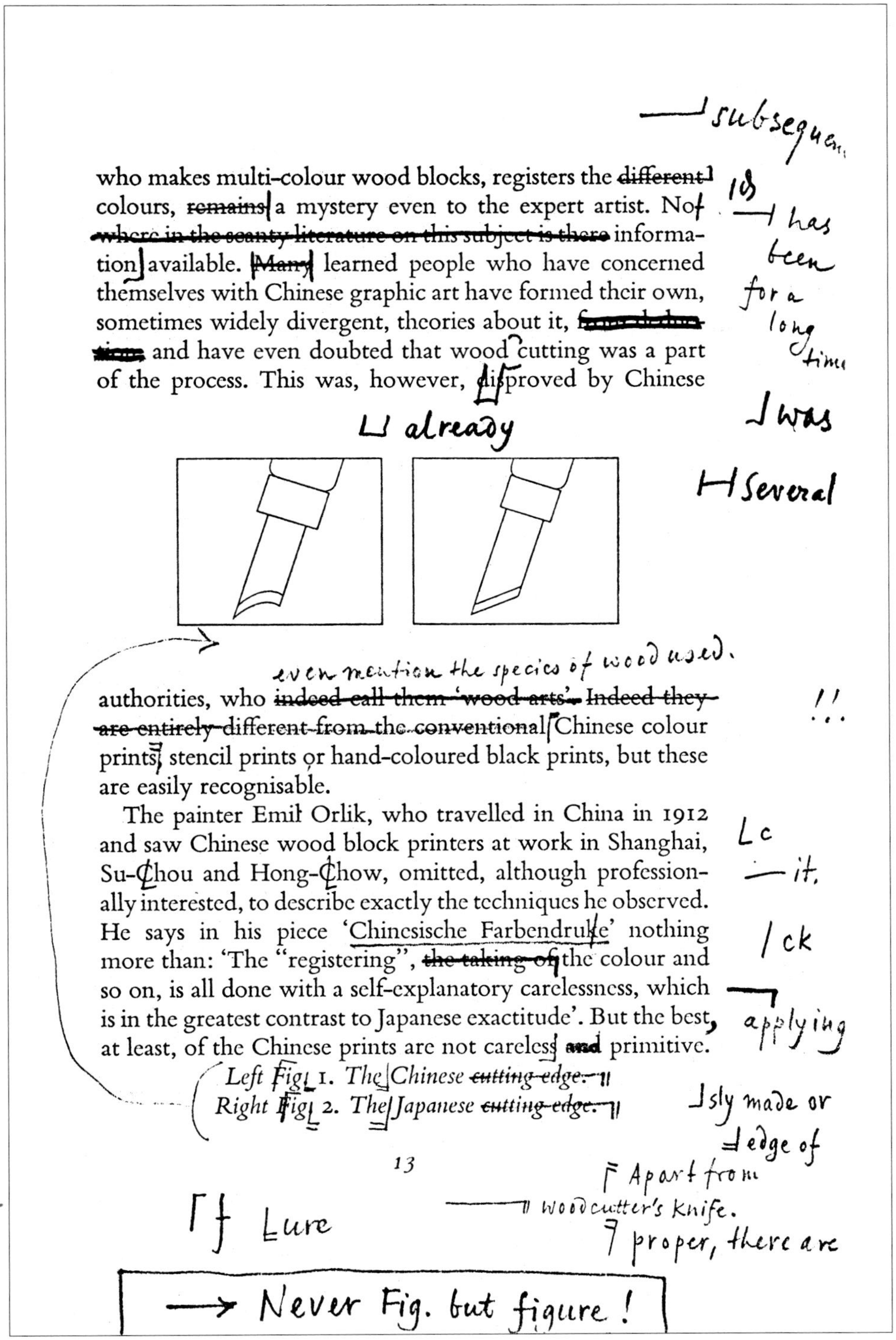

Two pages of the English translation with corrections in Tschichold's hand. On the last page he wrote: 'The whole was "edited", "translated", and composed by imbeciles. J.T.'

who makes multi-colour wood blocks, registers the ~~different~~
colours, ~~remains~~ a mystery even to the expert artist. No~~t~~
~~where in the scanty literature on this subject is there~~ informa-
tion available. ~~Many~~ learned people who have concerned
themselves with Chinese graphic art have formed their own,
sometimes widely divergent, theories about it, ~~for a long~~
~~time~~ and have even doubted that wood cutting was a part
of the process. This was, however, disproved by Chinese

[handwritten margin notes: "— subsequent", "is", "has been for a long time", "was", "several"]

[handwritten: "⊔ already"]

[handwritten above authorities line: "even mention the species of wood used."]

authorities, who ~~indeed call them 'wood-arts'. Indeed they~~
~~are entirely different from the conventional~~ Chinese colour
prints, stencil prints or hand-coloured black prints, but these
are easily recognisable.

The painter Emil Orlik, who travelled in China in 1912
and saw Chinese wood block printers at work in Shanghai,
Su-Chou and Hong-Chow, omitted, although profession-
ally interested, to describe exactly the techniques he observed.
He says in his piece 'Chinesische Farbendruke' nothing
more than: 'The "registering", ~~the taking of~~ the colour and
so on, is all done with a self-explanatory carelessness, which
is in the greatest contrast to Japanese exactitude'. But the best,
at least, of the Chinese prints are not careless ~~and~~ primitive.

[handwritten margin notes: "Lc", "— it.", "/ ck", "applying"]

Left Fig. 1. The Chinese ~~cutting edge.~~
Right Fig. 2. The Japanese ~~cutting edge.~~

[handwritten margin notes: "!!", "...", "sly made or", "edge of"]

13

[handwritten: "⌐f Lure", "⌐ Apart from", "woodcutter's knife.", "proper, there are"]

[handwritten box: "→ Never Fig. but figure!"]

Cover of booklet written and designed by
Tschichold on the ampersand ('Et-Zeichen'),
1954, actual size. Original in black and brown
on cream paper.

JAN TSCHICHOLD

FORMENWANDLUNGEN

&

DER ET-ZEICHEN

Jan Tschichold

Geschichte

der

Schrift

in

Bildern

Hauswedell

Jacket design for *History of Type in Pictures*, 1961, reduced. Original in black and terracotta on cream.

JÜRG BÄR

———

Die

Funktionen

der

Vitamine

VII

Der Bedarf an Vitaminen

Der Vitaminbedarf des Menschen hängt von verschiedenen Faktoren ab und ist nicht von konstanter Größe. Da Kinder einen kleineren Körper als die Erwachsenen mit Vitaminen zu versorgen haben, ist ihr Bedarf in absoluten Zahlen geringer, relativ jedoch ist er größer, denn Wachstum und Entwicklung verlangen eine erhöhte Zufuhr. Das gilt nicht nur für die Vitamine, die an diesen Vorgängen unmittelbar beteiligt sind, sondern auch für die übrigen Vitamine. Ebenso liegt es auf der Hand, daß schwangere und stillende Frauen einen erhöhten Vitaminbedarf haben, da sie ja nicht nur sich selbst, sondern auch noch das herankeimende Lebewesen bzw. den Säugling versorgen müssen. Besonders hohe Dosen, die oft ein Vielfaches des normalen Tagesbedarfes betragen, werden zu therapeutischen Zwecken gegeben. Die Vitaminbehandlung muß von zwei verschiedenen Standpunkten aus betrachtet werden: Sie ist einmal indiziert, wenn Hypovitaminosen oder Avitaminosen vorliegen, das heißt wenn eigentliche Vitamin-Mangelkrank-

261

Cover and text page of booklet in the series designed for the Swiss pharmaceutical firm of Hoffmann-La Roche, 1964, actual size.

Cover of booklet for Hoffmann-La Roche, 1964, reduced. Original printed in black and red on green card.

Pathophysiology of the Emotions

A consideration of functional,
anatomical and pharmacological aspects,
together with therapeutic implications;
with special reference to ‹Librium›

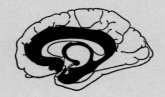

Block in full size.

A „must"

4½

3½

Schönste liebe mich

Deutsche Liebesgedichte
aus dem Barock und dem Rokoko

Mit farbigen Wiedergaben
acht alter Spitzenbildchen

Verlag Lambert Schneider,
Heidelberg

1957.

Jan Tschichold: Title, 1957. Full size.

Border to be set, 24 by 38 pica ems.
Please observe upper and left-hand margins
as indicated, precisely! Use the same thickness of line
as in upper part of
Do not centre it.

Jan Tschichold, Hon. R.D.I. the
CH 6611 BERZONA Onsernone illu-
stration
(Schweiz, Switzerland)

Notes on a title page
designed by Tschichold,
worth reading carefully.

ERASMUS VON ROTTERDAM

DAS LOB DER TORHEIT

Übersetzt von Alfred Hartmann
Mit den Holbeinschen Randzeichnungen
herausgegeben von Emil Major

MCMLXVI

BIRKHÄUSER VERLAG BASEL
UND STUTTGART

Gleichheit herauskommt? Sie jedoch, stolz auf diese Kindereien, rümpfen die Nase über die andern, aber auch über einander, und Männer, die sich als Träger apostolischer Liebe geben, erfüllen die ganze Welt mit Geschrei, wenn eine Kutte anders gegürtet oder etwas dunkler gefärbt ist. Manche nehmen es so streng mit der Religion, daß sie als Oberkleid nur Wolle tragen, als Unterkleid nur Linnen; andere dagegen sind außen linnen und innen wollen. Noch andere rühren an Geld sowenig wie an Gift – nur an den Becher und an ein Weib zu rühren versagen sie sich mitnichten. 127

Und endlich steckt in allen ein außergewöhnlicher Trieb, in ihrer Lebensweise ja etwas Besonderes zu haben, doch nicht, um Christo ähnlich, vielmehr um untereinander unähnlich zu sein. So beruht denn ein gut Teil ihres Glückes auf ihren Namen: den einen macht es Spaß, sich Strickträger zu heißen, wobei sie sich erst noch scheiden in Coletaner, Minoriten, Minimiten und Bullisten; andere nennen sich lieber Benediktiner

Title page and p.127 of a Birkhäuser edition of Erasmus's *The Praise of Folly*, 1966, actual size. Illustrations in the style of Holbein's etchings.

DIE

FÜRSTIN VON CLEVE

VON

MARIE MADELEINE

GRÄFIN VON

LAFAYETTE

IM VERLAG ZUM EINHORN

ZU BASEL

DIE

Fürstin von Cleve

VON

MARIE MADELEINE

GRÄFIN VON

LAFAYETTE

IM

VERLAG ZUM EINHORN

ZU BASEL

DIE FÜRSTIN VON

CLEVE

VON

Marie Madeleine Gräfin

von Lafayette

Im Verlag zum Einhorn

BASEL

Three versions of an imaginary title page, from pp.82-7 of *The Form of the Book*, translated from Tschichold's German by Hajo Hadeler, Hartley & Marks/Lund Humphries, 1991.

The captions:

'Figure 14. An imaginary title page, well set, but it lacks originality.

Figure 15. The same title page, using unspaced lowercase letters in the major line. Much better than figure 14.

Figure 16. Finally, this kind of typography captures the spirit of the time. But it isn't as simple as it looks.'

Jan Tschichold, Buchtitel 1945.
Das Thema fordert einen verzierten Titel. Rechts: Buchtitel mit demselben Text in »funktionaler« Typographie. Im Hinblick auf den Inhalt völlig ungeeignet.

Bills Augen ein Zugeständnis sein, hält er doch wohl noch immer die Grotesk für die beste, weil »zeitgemäße« Schrift. Die Grotesk ist keine neue Schrift. Ihr Charakter ist im ersten Drittel des 19. Jahrhunderts aufgekommen. Sie ist vor allem eine Titelschrift und nur in kurzen Abschnitten als Werkschrift brauchbar, da sie sich, mangels hinreichender Artikulation durch die unentbehrlichen Endungen und infolge ihrer monotonen Strichstärke nicht gut lesen läßt. Ihre Einfachheit ist eine scheinbare; sie entspricht dem unentwickelten Wahrnehmungsvermögen von ABC-Schützen, die buchstabieren müssen und deren ungeübten Augen die echten Buchstabenformen der Druckschrift ebenso kompliziert erscheinen wie etwa die Schulhandschrift der Zwölfjährigen.

Es ist kein bloßer Zufall, daß die meisten Jünger der funktionalen Typo-

27

The caption reads:

'Jan Tschichold, title page 1945. The subject demands a decorated title page. Right: title page with the same text in "functional" typography. Quite out of keeping with the subject.'

From *Beiheft die neue typographie* (with essays on the history of the book by Werner Doede, Jan Tschichold, and Gerd Fleischmann). Brinkmann & Bose, Berlin, 1987.

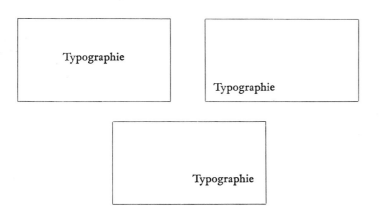

empfinden mindestens krasse Verfehlungen. So zeigen die beiden oberen Beispiele die traditionelle und eine mißglückte Stellung einer Zeile in der Papierfläche. Das dritte Beispiel ist unkonventionell, aber gut. Die entstehenden Ränder und Intervalle sollten stets deutlich verschieden sein, wenn eine gute asymmetrische Form entstehen soll:

Typographie	Typographie
Falsch	*Richtig*

Stellen wir die Zeile so, daß zwei Ränder gleich sind, so ist die Wirkung längst nicht so gut wie in der richtigen Lösung. Eine Buchseite, deren weiße Ränder gleich breit sind, wirkt ebenso schlecht.

71

A page from Tschichold's *Erfreuliche Drucksachen durch gute Typographie* ('Pleasant printing through good typography'), Ravensburg, 1960.

The text states:

'In typography it is wrong to take a line of type from a normal position and place it anywhere asymmetrically. We see this often done today with poor results. The two upper examples show a traditional and a mistaken placing. The third example is unconventional, but good. Margins and intervals must always be clearly different, if a good asymmetric form is to be created. If the two margins are equal, the result is not nearly so effective as the example on the right. A page of type with equal margins will also look wrong.'

SÜDKURIER

Capital letters drawn by Tschichold for
a periodical, 1968.

     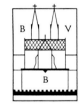

Symbols designed by Tschichold.
From left to right:
Poeschel & Trepte, Leipzig, 1927
Insel-Verlag, Leipzig, 1931
Der Bücherkreis, Berlin, 1931
Edith Tschichold, 1951
Birkhäuser Verlag, Basel, 1941
Burg-Verlag, Basel, 1942
Heinrich Majer Verlag, Basel, 1951
F. Hoffmann-La Roche, Basel, 1957

Mai · Mai · Maggio

1 20 3

Mittwoch · Mercredi · Mercoledì

4 5 6

7 8 9

Figures for a calendar. Note the shaping of the 'zero' and that the same figure is used for '6' and '9'. Undated.

JAN TSCHICHOLD

DAS ALPHABET DES
DAMIANUS MOYLLUS

PARMA UM 1483

ÜBERREICHT
VON BUCHERER, KURRUS & CO
PAPIERE EN GROS · BASEL

DER anfang der wiederbelebung der römifchen infchriftenbuchftaben und der karolingifchen bücherfchrift wird durch den kodex Vat. lat. 6852 bezeichnet, der in der bibliothek des Vatikans aufbewahrt wird. Er ftammt von der hand des FELICE FELICIANO (1433 bis 1479) und ift nicht fpäter als 1460 entftanden. Felice Feliciano, fohn eines weinzöllners, lebte in Verona und war kalligraph und altertumsforfcher. In der erwähnten *handfchrift* verfucht er, die fchönheit der römifchen lapidarfchrift in geometrifchen formeln feftzulegen. Sein wertvolles werk, eine unterfuchung, die nicht gedruckt wurde, ift 1960 von Hans Marderfteig in einem herrlichen buche[2] erfchloffen worden. ¶ Die ältefte *gedruckte* vorlagenfolge ähnlicher geometrifcher buchftabenkonftruktionen ift erft um das jahr 1483 in Parma entftanden. Sie ift fchwerlich als eigentliches buch geplant worden, denn das einzige exemplar, das auf uns gekommen ift, ift einfeitig auf fechs bogen gedruckt, deren jeder vier buchftaben enthält, ift nicht geheftet und enthält keinen titel. Am fuße der feite mit dem Z lieft man nur ‹Imprefum parme per Damianum Moyllum: Parmenfem›, ohne angabe eines jahres. Es wurde von Leo S. Olfchki entdeckt und ift von Stanley Morifon[1] kurz nachher, 1927, eingehend erörtert und in kleiner auflage publiziert worden. Diefes felten gewordene fakfimile liegt unferem neudruck zugrunde, dem erften in deutfcher fprache. ¶ Die konftruktionen follten vermutlich als unterrichtshilfen dienen. Ihr verfaffer war

5

Title page and first text page of Tschichold's *Das Alphabet des Damianus Moyllus, Parma um 1483*, Basel, 1971. Note the use of signs to mark paragraphs. There are only six text pages; in a longer book these paragraph marks might become disturbing. Slightly reduced.

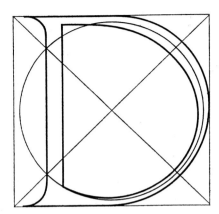

Das D entfteht aus kreis und viereck. Der fenk‚
rechte fchaft fteht rechts vom fchnittpunkt oben
und unten. Der körper nimmt wie die andern
rundungen auf derfelben linie zu, auf der alle
andern kreisteile zunehmen. Die obere linie mit
dem winkel über dem kreife foll halb fo dick fein
wie der fchaft, die untere folgt dem kreife. Der
fchwächere teil des körpers, den die andere dia‚
gonale trifft, mufs halb fo dick fein wie ein dicker
ftrich. Alle buchftaben folgen diefer regel.

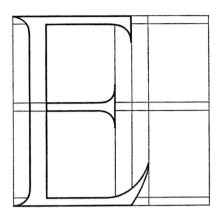

Das E entfteht aus dem viereck. Die ftärke des
grundftrichs ift ein zwölftel der höhe. Die quer‚
ftriche follen halb fo dick fein wie der grundftrich.
Der mittlere querftrich ift um die ftärke des grund‚
ftrichs kürzer als die andern, er foll oberhalb der
mittellinie des vierecks liegen.

Two illustrated pages from *Moyllus*. The
letters are printed in a pale blue-mauve.

Tschichold's reconstruction of an engraving in wood or metal of 'The oldest printed poster made for an established tradesman: Paris, *circa* 1560'. Reduced. See p.15.

Salomon

Tschichold's reconstruction of a gothic wood type from a worn proof in Christopher Plantin's office in Antwerp, c.1570. Reduced. Both upper and lower case were shown in a four-page leaflet, 370 x 260 mm, printed for friends at Christmas 1958 by the paper firm Bucherer, Kurrus & Co, Basel.

JAN TSCHICHOLD

DER CHINESISCHE STEMPEL:

URSPRUNG DES BUCHDRUCKS

ÜBERREICHT
VON BUCHERER, KURRUS & CO
PAPIERE EN GROS · BASEL

Der älteste und einfachste Buchdruck der Welt ist der FINGERABDRUCK. Die leicht erhabenen Linienmuster der menschlichen Hand, der Finger und des Daumens sind sicherlich schon in der Vorzeit dann und wann bemerkt worden. Viel später erst lernte man, daß diese Papillarlinienmuster oder Hautleistenfiguren bei jedem Menschen verschieden sind. Ein Stückchen Tonerde chinesischen Ursprungs hat sich erhalten, das auf der einen Seite einen deutlichen Daumenabdruck und auf der andern den vertieften farblosen Abdruck eines chinesischen Namenssiegels zeigt. Es mag als Beweismittel zu einer Urkunde, einem Brief oder einer Umhüllung gehört haben und ist spätestens im dritten Jahrhundert vor unserer Zeitrechnung angefertigt worden[7]. Der Daumenabdruck sollte gewiß die Glaubwürdigkeit des Siegels erhärten. Will man in ihm nicht bloß einen Anwesenheitsbeweis des Unterzeichners sehn[3], so belegt er, daß man schon in so früher Zeit in China empirisch die unfälschbare Individualität des Fingerabdrucks erkannt hatte. Laufer[7] meint, originale Ideen seien so selten, daß es höchst unwahrscheinlich wäre, daß eine komplexe Folge von Ideen, wie sie der Vorgang des Fingerabdrucks ist, einige Male von verschiedenen Nationen oder Menschen unabhängig entwickelt wurde. ✳ Der Fingerabdruck lieferte auch die Idee der ältesten künstlichen Hochdruckform, des STEMPELS. Es gibt einige alte und neueste chinesische Stempel, die keine Schriftzeichen, sondern das Papillarlinienmuster eines Fingers enthalten. Einen solchen Stempel zeigt die Abbildung am Anfang dieser Seite. In alten Zeiten hat ein Befehlshaber dem Stempel oft seinen Fingerabdruck hinzugefügt. Noch heutzutage drückt in China ein Mann, der keinen Stempel führt, dafür den eingefärbten Finger auf. ✳ Das chinesische Wort für ‹Stempel› ist yin. Das Zeichen yin ist in zwei verschiedenen Formen auf dem Umschlag und dem Titelblatt dieses Aufsatzes, in Siegelschrift geschrieben, abgebildet. Die heutige Form des Zeichens ist 印. Yin bedeutet aber auch ‹Buchdruck›. Dies besagt, daß China die Erfin-

5

Title page and first text page of Tschichold's booklet on 'Chinese blocks: the origin of book printing', privately printed, 1972. Slightly reduced.

Jan and Edith Tschichold with Antonia McLean
(centre), Berzona, 1971. Photo by the author.

Jan and Edith Tschichold on the way to Leipzig,
May 1971. Photo by the author.

CHRONOLOGY

1902   Born 2 April in Leipzig, eldest son of Franz Tschichold, sign painter and lettering artist, and his wife Maria, née Zapff.

1914   'BUGRA' (International Exhibition of the Graphic Arts) in Leipzig was an important event, and the 'Hall of Culture', which remained open after the main exhibition closed, laid the foundations of Tschichold's education.

1916-19   Student at Teacher Training College in Grimma, near Leipzig.

1919-21   Tschichold, aged seventeen, was accepted into the class of Professor Hermann Delitsch at the Academy for Graphic Arts and Book Production in Leipzig, and learned calligraphy, engraving, etching, wood-engraving and book-binding. Delitsch was above all a calligrapher, and introduced Tschichold to the writing masters of the Italian Renaissance.

1921-3   Worked in School of Arts and Crafts, Dresden, under Heinrich Wieynck, and was then appointed assistant in charge of evening classes in lettering at the Leipzig Academy, by Walter Tiemann, whose special student he became.

1923-5   Freelance typographer and calligrapher in Leipzig.

1923   First Bauhaus exhibition at Weimar, visited by Tschichold.

1925   Tschichold's 'Elementare Typographie' published as a special number of *Typographische Mitteilungen*, Leipzig.

1925-6   Freelance work in Berlin.

1926   Married Edith Kramer. Invited by Paul Renner to German Master Printers' School, Munich, to teach typography and calligraphy.

1926-33   Taught *c.*30 hours a week in Munich.

1928   Tschichold's first book, *Die neue Typographie*, published in Berlin.

1929   Birth of son Peter.

1933   Placed in 'protective custody' by the Nazis and lost his job in Munich. Emigrated to Basel, Switzerland.

1933-40   Part-time work for publisher Benno Schwabe in Basel.

1935   Exhibition of Tschichold's typography in the London office of Lund Humphries Printers. Publication of *Typographische Gestaltung*.

1937   Paper read to Double Crown Club, London.

1941-6   Typographer to Birkhäuser Verlag, Basel.

1942   Awarded Basel citizenship.

1947-9   Typographer for Penguin Books, London.

1949   Elected Honorary Member of the Double Crown Club, London.

1950-4   Freelance work in Basel.

1955-67   Typographic adviser to the pharmaceutical firm F. Hoffmann-La Roche in Basel.

1964   Began work on design of 'Sabon' typeface.

1965   Elected Honorary Royal Designer for Industry (Hon. RDI), London. Gutenberg Prize of Leipzig.

1967   Visited USA. First sizes of 'Sabon' appeared. Moved to Berzona.

1974   Died on 11 August in Locarno Hospital.

SELECT BIBLIOGRAPHY

WORKS BY TSCHICHOLD

Die neue Typographie, Berlin, 1928 (1st edition).

Die neue Typographie, Brinkmann & Bose, Berlin, 1987 (facsimile reprint).

[Published in English as *The New Typography*, translated by Ruari McLean with an Introduction by Robin Kinross, University of California Press, 1995.]

Typografische Entwurfstechnik, Stuttgart, 1932.

[Published in English as *How to Draw Layouts*, translated by Ruari McLean, Merchiston Publishing, Edinburgh, 1991 (limited edition of 150 copies).]

Typographische Gestaltung, Benno Schwabe, Basel, 1935.

[Published in English as *Asymmetric Typography*, translated by Ruari McLean, Reinhold, New York and Faber and Faber, London, 1967.]

Designing Books, Wittenborn, Schultz, New York, 1951 [short text and 58 reproductions, some in colour].

Ausgewählte Aufsätze über Fragen der Gestalt des Buches und der Typographie, Birkhäuser, Basel, 1975.

[Published in English as *The Form of the Book: Essays on the Morality of Good Design*, translated by Hajo Hadeler, Hartley & Marks, Vancouver and Lund Humphries Publishers, London, 1991.]

Schriften 1925-1974, Brinkmann & Bose, Berlin, 2 volumes, 1991 and 1992.
[A collection of Tschichold's articles with illustrations.]

BOOKS ABOUT TSCHICHOLD

Jan Tschichold: Typograph und Schriftentwerfer 1902-1974. Das Lebenswerk, Kunstgewerbemuseum Zurich, 1976.
[Lists everything written by or about Tschichold up to 1976, with short articles by Jost Hochuli, Kurt Weidemann, Berthold Wolpe and Hans Peter Willberg.]

[Published in English as *Jan Tschichold: Typographer and Type Designer 1902-1974*, translated by Ruari McLean, National Library of Scotland, Edinburgh, 1982.]

Ruari McLean, *Jan Tschichold: Typographer*, Lund Humphries Publishers, London, and David R. Godine, Boston, Massachusetts, 1975.

J.T. Johannes Tschichold, Iwan Tschichold, Jan Tschichold, edited and published by Philipp Luidl, Munich, 1976.

Leben und Werk des Typographen Jan Tschichold, with an Introduction by Werner Klemke, Verlag der Kunst, Dresden, 1977.

Hans Schmoller, *Two Titans, Mardersteig and Tschichold: A Study in Contrasts*, The Typophiles, New York, 1990.

Paul Barnes (ed.), *Jan Tschichold: Reflections and Reappraisals*, with contributions by twenty important designers and Edith Tschichold, limited edition of 200 copies printed by Stinehour Press, Vermont and published by Typoscope, New York, 1995.

INDEX